How Video Works

How Video Works

Marcus Weise
Diana Weynand

AMSTERDAM • BOSTON • HEIDELBERG • LONDON
NEW YORK • OXFORD • PARIS • SAN DIEGO
SAN FRANCISCO • SINGAPORE • SYDNEY • TOKYO

Focal Press is an imprint of Elsevier

ELSEVIER

Focal
Press

Focal Press is an imprint of Elsevier
200 Wheeler Road, Burlington, MA 01803, USA
Linacre House, Jordan Hill, Oxford OX2 8DP, UK

∞ Recognizing the importance of preserving what has been written, Elsevier prints
its books on acid-free paper whenever possible.

Library of Congress Cataloging-in-Publication Data
Weise, Marcus
   How video works/Marcus Weise, Diana Weynand
      p. cm
Includes index.
ISBN-13: 978-0-240-80614-3   ISBN-10: 0-240-80614-X
[1. Home video systems.] I. Weynand, Diana. II. Title
   TK9961. W45 2004
   778.59—dc22

ISBN-13: 978-0-240-80614-3
ISBN-10: 0-240-80614-X

2004002307

British Library Cataloguing-in-Publication Data
A catalogue record for this book is available from the British Library.

For information on all Focal Press publications
visit our website at www.focalpress.com

05 06 07 08 10 9 8 7 6 5 4 3 2

Printed in the United States of America

Contents

Acknowledgments

The authors would like to thank the following:

Shirley Craig for helping to make this book a possibility, and through Weynand Training, supporting this book's predecessor, "Video Theory and Operations," over the past several years.

Diane Wright, for her tireless efforts in providing research, writing contributions, digital photography, and many graphic illustrations in this book. We appreciate your support of this project over the years.

And Jerzy Gorczyca, Assistant Maintenance Supervisor, CBS Television City in Hollywood, for reading and providing notes to the first draft of this book, and Vance Piccin for his valuable feedback.

From Marcus Weise:

I would like to take this opportunity to express my thanks and appreciation to Diana Weynand for her extraordinary friendship, kindness, and help through these many years, and to my Golden Haired Angel who is with me always and in whose spirit all things are possible.

From Diana Weynand:

I would like to thank the Fielder women—my aunts, Billie, Koko, Mary, and Jewel, and my mother, Dee—for showing me, through their personal experiences, what it is to live a resilient life.

CHAPTER 1

Introduction

Since the development of broadcast cameras and television sets in the early 1940s, video has slowly become more and more a part of everyday life. In the early 50s, it was a treat simply to have a television set in one's own home. In the 60s, television brought the world live coverage of an astronaut walking on the moon. With the 70s, the immediacy of television brought the events of the Vietnam War into living rooms. In the 21st century, with additional modes of delivery such as satellite and cable, video has developed into the primary source of world communication.

Video Evolution

Just as the use of this medium has changed over the years, so has its physical evolution. The video signal started as analog and has developed into digital with different types of digital formats, including some for the digital enthusiast at home. When television was first created, cameras and television sets required a great deal of room to house the original tube technology of the analog world. In today's digital society, camera size and media continue to get smaller as the quality continues to improve.

Today, a video image is conveyed using digital components and chips rather than tubes. Although the equipment has changed, some of the processes involved in the origination of the video signal have remained the same. This makes the progression of video from analog to digital not only interesting to study, but crucial in providing a foundation of knowledge upon which the current digital video world operates. So much of the digital technology of today is the way it is because it evolved from analog *to* digital.

Analog and Digital

No matter how digital the equipment is that is used to capture an image, the eyes and ears see the final result as analog. All information from the physical world is analog. A cloud floating by, an ocean wave, and the sounds of a marching band all exist within a spectrum of frequencies that comprise human experience. This spectrum of frequencies can be converted to digital data, or zeros and ones. Human beings, however, do not process digital information, and eventually what a human being sees or hears must be converted back from digital data to an analog form. Even with a digital home receiver, the zeros and ones of the digital signal must be reproduced as an analog experience (Figure 1.1).

In the early days of television, video was captured, recorded, and reproduced as an analog signal. The primary medium for storage was videotape, which is a magnetic medium. The primary system for reproduction was mechanical, using a videotape machine. Videotape, which was developed based on mechanical concepts, is a linear medium. This means that information can only be recorded or reproduced in the order in which it was created. With the advent of digital, the primary system for signal reproduction

Analog Sine Wave   **Digital Square Wave**   **Analog Sine Wave**

Figure 1.1 Analog and Digital Domains

has become solid-state electronics, incorporating servers and computers. This change has created a file-based system. File-based systems allow random access to information without respect to the order in which it was produced or its placement within the storage medium.

Video Applications

Facilities such as cable or broadcast stations, as well as production or post-production companies, are constantly transmitting and receiving video signals. They generally have a number of devices that can be used to capture and reproduce a video signal, such as videotape recorders (VTRs), videocassette recorders (VCRs), computer disks or hard drives, servers, and so on. Figure 1.2 shows different ways in which a VTR, VCR, or computer might be used to capture, transmit, or reproduce a video signal.

About This Book

To create a complete picture of the video process, and answer the question of "How Video Works," this book will begin by examining the analog video signal. Digital video technology is a direct evolution from the analog system. Having the knowledge of the analog system provides a firm foundation before moving into a discussion of digital.

While this book is designed to cover the process of creating a video signal, storing it, and transmitting it in a professional environment, the same information and concepts apply to any video tool, including consumer equipment.

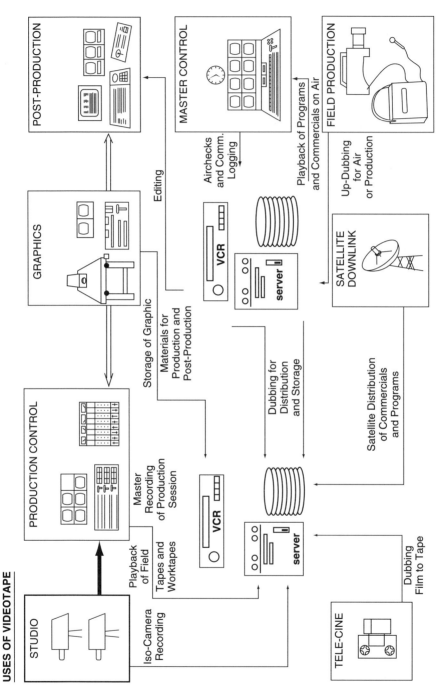

Figure 1.2 Uses of Video

CHAPTER 2

Electronic Photography

Video starts with a camera, as all picture taking does. In still and motion-picture film photography, there is a mechanical system that controls the amount of light falling on a strip of film. Light is then converted into a pattern of varying chemical densities on the film. As a physical medium, film can be cut, spliced, edited, and manipulated in other ways, as well.

In electronic photography, the light from an object goes through a lens, as it does in film photography. On the other side of the video camera lens, however, light is converted to an image by an electronic process as opposed to a mechanical or chemical process. The medium for this conversion has changed over the years. It began with tube cameras and has progressed to completely electronic components. The tube cameras will be discussed first and the section following will cover this process as it occurs in digital cameras.

Tube Cameras

In a video tube camera, the lens focuses the image on the face of a pickup tube inside the camera. The face of the pickup tube is known as the *target* (Figure 2.1). The target is light sensitive, like a piece of film. When light shines on the face of the target, it conducts electricity in proportion to the amount of light that is striking its surface. Without light on the face of the target, the target resists the flow of electricity.

A stream of electrons, called the *beam*, coming from the back end of the tube, scans back and forth across the face of the target

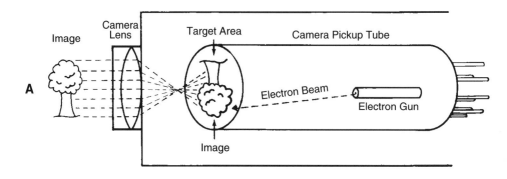

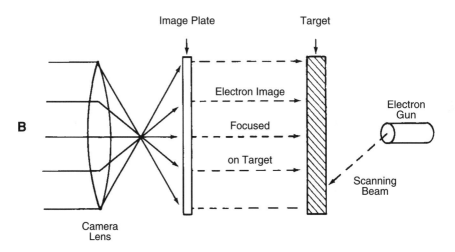

Figure 2.1 A, Camera Focusing on Image and **B**, Tube Camera Target Area

on the inside of the pickup tube. The electrical current generated is either allowed to pass from the target to the camera output, or it is not allowed to pass, depending on the amount of resistance at the face of the target. The amount of resistance varies depending on how much light is shining on the target. In every video camera, there are adjustments for the beam intensity and the sensitivity of the face of the target. The target acts as either an insulator when not exposed to light, or as a conductor when light shines on its face. The electrical signal that flows from the target is, in effect, the electronic recreation of the light coming from the scene at which the camera is aimed.

Scanning the Image

Scanning the image begins with the beam of electrons sweeping back and forth across the inside face of the target. Where the electron beam strikes the face of the target, it illuminates an area the same size as the electron beam. This "dot" of electron illumination is called the *aperture* (Figure 2.2).

The dot or aperture is the smallest size that an element of picture information can be. The larger the aperture, the less detail in the

Scanned Image   Reproduced Image

Figure 2.2 Scanning and Reproducing an Image

picture. The smaller the aperture, the more detail in the picture. Dot size, or *beam aperture*, is comparable to drawing with large, blunt crayons or fine-tipped pens. Crayons can outline shapes or color them in. A fine-tipped pen can add texture and small highlights to a drawing. In a digital video signal, these picture elements are called *pixels*, short for picture elements (Figure 2.3).

Figure 2.3 Magnified Picture Elements

The electron beam must always be kept perpendicular to the face of the target. If it were not perpendicular as it scanned back and forth, then only one line in the center of the television image would be in focus. The lines closest to the top and bottom of the picture would be badly distorted, because at these angles the aperture dot would be shaped like an ellipse.

In the camera pickup tube, there are *horizontal deflection coils* and *vertical deflection coils*. They move the electron beam across the target as well as up and down (Figure 2.4). A series of grids inside the neck of the pickup tube focuses the electron beam and keeps the beam always perpendicular to the target. This keeps the aperture as small as possible and therefore, the image as sharp as possible.

In the television system that is used in the United States, the electron beam will scan back and forth across the target 525 times in each television frame. Thus each frame in the television signal is composed of *525 scan lines*. It does not matter what size the camera

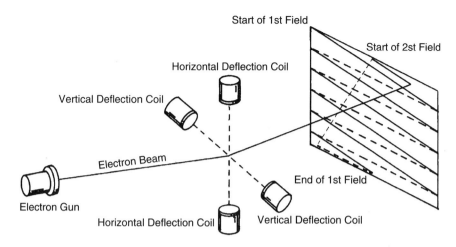

Figure 2.4 Deflection Coils

is or what size the pickup tube or monitor is. The total number of lines scanned from the top of the frame to the bottom of the frame will always be 525.

The image created in the video camera has now been turned into an electronic signal of varying voltages. As an electronic signal, the television image can be carried by cables, recorded on videotape machines, or even transmitted through the air.

Displaying the Image

There is a peculiar problem that is caused by lenses. A right-side-up image coming through the face of a lens will be inverted, or turned upside down, as it comes out of that lens. In film, this is not a serious problem. Although the image is recorded upside down on the film, when it goes back through a lens during projection, it is once again inverted, and the image on the movie screen becomes right side up.

In video, the camera lens causes the image to be focused upside down on the face of the target (see Figure 2.1). There is no lens in front of a television monitor or receiver to flip the upside-down image right side up again. The television image is inverted by scanning the image in the camera from the bottom to the top, instead of from the top down. On the receiver, or monitor, the scan is from top to bottom. This way the image appears right side up on the monitor.

The varying voltages generated by the camera can be converted back into light. This electrical energy powers an *electron gun* in the television receiver or monitor. That gun sends a stream of electrons to the face of the picture tube in the receiver. Changing voltages in the video signal cause chemical phosphors on the inside face of the receiver tube to glow with intensity in direct proportion to the amount of voltage. The image that originated in the tube camera is thus recreated, line by line. Motion and detail are all reproduced.

CCD Cameras

The majority of tube cameras have been replaced by cameras using digital technology. Rather than using a pickup tube to turn the light into an electrical signal, the incoming light is focused on a light-sensitive chip (Figure 2.5). The chip is a *charge-coupled device*, or CCD, which is where this type of camera gets its name. CCD cameras are also referred to as chip cameras.

A CCD is a chip that contains an area, or site, covered with thousands, and in some instances millions, of tiny *capacitors* or *condensers* (devices for storing electrical energy). Consumer digital still cameras have chips that can contain as many as five million sites, or five megapixels. This chip came out of the technology that was developed for EPROMS (Erasable Programmable Read Only Memory). They are used for computer software where updates or changes can occur. When the information is burned onto an EPROM, it is meant to be semi-permanent. It is erasable only under high-intensity ultraviolet light.

In a CCD camera, the light information that is converted to electrical energy is deposited on sites on the chip. Unlike an EPROM, however, it is easily removed or changed. The sites are tiny condensers that hold an electrical charge and are separated from each other by insulating material. This prevents the charge from leaking off. The chip is very efficient and can hold the information for extended periods of time.

The charge can be released and then replaced by the next set of charges. This type of technology has been useful in audio for digital echo devices. When sound is fed through one or more of these devices, the original audio is heard first. Fractions of a second later, the chips read out their signals and an echo is heard. The number and depth of the echoes, as well as the length of time between them, is fully controllable.

Camera Chips

Inside the chip camera, light coming through the lens is focused on a chip (Figure 2.5). In the case of cameras using multiple chips, light entering the camera goes through a *beam splitter* and is then focused onto the chips, rather than passing through a pickup tube or tubes. A beam splitter is an optical device that takes the light coming in through the lens and divides or splits it. It directs the light through filters that filter out all but one color for each of the chips. One chip sees only red light, one only blue, and one only green. The filters are called *dichroic* because they filter out two of the three colors. These chips are photo-sensitive, integrated circuits.

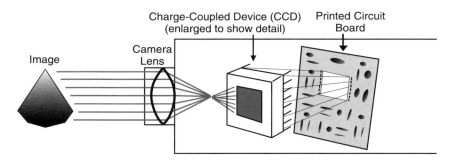

Figure 2.5 CCD Camera Focused on Image

When light strikes the chip, it charges the chip's sites with electrical energy in proportion to the amount of light that strikes it. In other words, the image that is focused on the chip is captured by the photo-sensitive surface as an electrical charge. This electrical charge is then read off the chip, site by site. The technology behind these chips allows them to shoot bright light without overloading. However, if the light is bright enough, the charge can spill over from one site to the next. This can causes the edges of an object within an image to *smear* or *lag*.

To prevent this, an optical grid or black screen is laid over the face of the chip so that between the light-sensitive sites there is both insulation and light-absorbing material. The same process is used in a video monitor where a *shadow mask* is used to prevent excess light from spilling over between adjacent phosphor groups on the screen, which would cause a blurring of the image.

To capture the information stored on the chip, the chip is scanned from site to site and the energy is discharged as this happens. A numerical value is assigned as each site is scanned, according to the amount of electrical energy present. This numerical information is converted to electrical energy at the output of the camera. This is part of the digitizing process, as the numerical value is converted to computer data for storage and transmission.

Lower-end consumer cameras typically have one CCD chip, while most professional or *pro-sumer* cameras have three. In consumer cameras, chips resemble the construction of TV receiver tubes. All three colors (red, green, and blue) are present on the one chip. There is no need for three chips and a beam splitter. Typically, the larger the size of the CCD or CCDs in the camera, the better the image quality. For example, a camera with a $\frac{2}{3}$-inch chip will capture a better quality image than a camera with a $\frac{1}{2}$-inch chip.

On professional cameras, there is one chip for each color: red, green, and blue (Figure 2.6). The *resolution* in these cameras is much greater, that is, the chips are better able to reproduce details in an image (resolution), which is determined by the number of sites on the chip. The more sites a chip has, the more detailed the

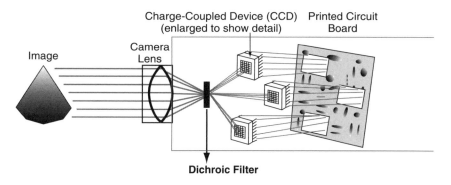

Figure 2.6 Three-Chip CCD

stored video information will be. The chip will also be more expensive. Also, through the camera's electronic-processing ability, the video image can be altered in several ways. For example, the resolution of an image can be increased without actually having more sites on the chip. An image can be enlarged digitally within the camera, beyond the optical ability of the lens. This same processing can also eliminate noise, or spurious information, and enhance the image.

During the digitizing process, certain artifacts can occur in the video that can be a problem. Through image processing in the camera, these artifacts can be blended to make them less noticeable. Sometimes these problems can also be overcome by changing a camera angle or altering the lighting.

Because of their small size and light weight, chip cameras have become very useful in field production, news work, documentaries, and even low-budget films. With their resistance to smearing and lagging and their ability to work in low-light situations, they have also found a use in studios. The pickup tubes and the scanning yokes needed to drive the tube cameras have been eliminated and replaced by CCDs.

CHAPTER 3

Scanning

When looking at a picture, such as a photograph or a drawing, the human eye takes the scene in all at once. The eye can move from spot to spot to examine details, but in essence, the entire picture is seen at one time. Likewise, when watching a film, the eye sees moving images go by on the screen. The illusion of motion is created by projecting many pictures or frames of film each second. Motion is perceived even though the film is made up of thousands of individual still pictures. Video is different from film in that a complete frame of video is broken up into component parts when it is created.

Video Lines

The electron beam inside a video camera transforms a light image into an electronic signal. Then, an electron beam within a video receiver or monitor causes chemicals called phosphors to glow so they transform the electrical signal back into light.

The specifications for this process were standardized by the NTSC (National Television Systems Committee) when the system was originally conceived in the late 1930s. The NTSC standard is used in North America and parts of Asia and Latin America. As other countries developed their own television systems, other video standards were created. Eastern and Western Europe use a system called PAL (Phase Alternate Line). France and the countries of the former Soviet Union use a system known as SECAM (Sequential Colour Avec Memoire, or Sequential Color with Memory).

For each NTSC video frame, the electron beam scans a total of 525 lines. There are 30 frames scanned each second, which means that a total of 15,750 lines (black and white video) are scanned each second (30 frames per second × 525 lines per frame). This rate is called the *line frequency*. The NTSC line frequency and frame rate changed with the addition of color. Both PAL and SECAM use 625 lines per frame at 25 frames per second. These two systems were developed with color already in existence and consequently did not require any additional changes. There are variations and combinations that attempt to combine the best elements of all of these standards.

Scanning 15,750 lines per second is so fast that the eye never notices the traveling beam. The video image is constantly refreshed as the electron beam scans the 525 lines in each frame. As soon as one frame is completely displayed, scanning begins on the next frame, so the whole process appears seamless to the viewer.

The electron beam in a video camera is caused to scan by electronic signals called drive pulses. *Horizontal drive pulses* move the beam back and forth; and *vertical drive pulses* move the horizontally scanning beam up the face of the pickup tube. These drive pulses are generated inside the camera.

Blanking

An electron beam scanning a picture tube is like an old typewriter. It works in only one direction. When it reaches the end of a line of video, it must *retrace* or go back to the other side of the screen to start the next line. Likewise, when it reaches the bottom of the image, it must retrace or go back to the top of the image to begin scanning the next frame (Figure 3.1).

The period of time during which the electron beam retraces to begin scanning or tracing the next line is part of a larger time interval called *horizontal blanking*. The period of time that the electron gun is retracing to the top of the image to begin scanning another frame is called *vertical blanking*. During horizontal or vertical blanking, the

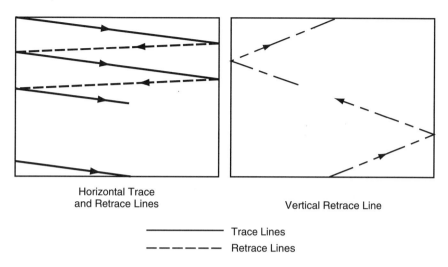

Horizontal Trace
and Retrace Lines

Vertical Retrace Line

——————— Trace Lines
— — — — — — Retrace Lines

Figure 3.1 Scanning and Retracing

beam of electrons is blanked out or turned off, so as not to cause any voltage to flow. This way the retrace is not visible.

The horizontal blanking interval is the separation between consecutive lines. The vertical blanking interval is the separation between consecutive frames. As the video image is integrated with other images, using equipment such as video editing systems or video switchers, the change from source to source occurs during the vertical blanking interval after a complete image has been drawn. This can be compared to splicing on the frame line of a film frame.

Horizontal blanking actually occurs a little before the beginning of each line of video information. Vertical blanking occurs after each frame. The video picture itself is referred to as *active video* (Figure 3.2). In the NTSC system, active video uses 480 out of the 525 lines contained in one frame. PAL and SECAM use 580 active lines out of the 625 total lines. Blanking functions as the picture frame around the active video. It is a necessary component of the TV signal, even though the electron beam is shut off. Blanking specifications are an important part of the picture specifications.

Figure 3.2 Video Frame

Persistence of Vision

Film is shot at 24 frames per second. However, if it were projected at that rate, a flickering quality to the moving image would be noticeable. The flickering is a result of the phenomenon that lets us perceive motion in a movie in the first place. That phenomenon is called *persistence of vision*.

Persistence of vision means that the retina, or light-sensitive portion of the human eye, retains the image exposed to it for a certain period of time. This image then fades as the eye waits to receive the next image. The threshold of retention is $\frac{1}{30}$ to $\frac{1}{32}$ of a second. If the images change on the retina at a rate slower than that, the eye sees the light and then the dark that follows. If the images change at a faster rate, the eye sees the images as continuous motion and not as individual images. This concept was the basis of a device developed in the 19th century called the Zoetrope (Figure 3.3). By viewing a series of still images through a small slit in a spinning wheel, the images appeared to move.

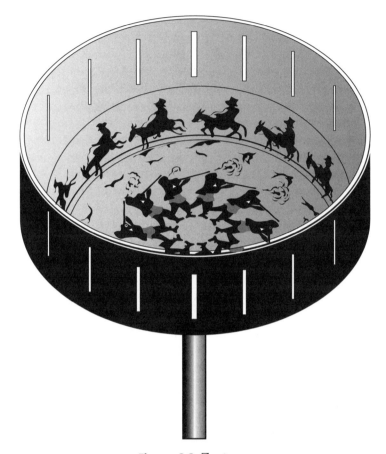

Figure 3.3 Zoetrope

In film, this concept is exploited by simply showing each frame twice. The picture in the gate of the film projector is held, and the shutter opens twice. Then the film moves to the next frame and the shutter again reveals the picture twice. In this way, 48 frames per second are shown while the projector runs at 24 frames per second, and the eye perceives smooth, continuous motion.

Fields

The 30-frames-per-second frame rate of video could potentially allow the flicker of the changing frames to be noticeable. Therefore, the frame rate needed to be increased. The simplest way to do this was to split the individual frames into two parts, creating 60 half-frames per second. These half-frames are called *fields*. Each field consists of alternate lines of a single frame.

The pickup tubes or the CCDs read out every other line of the video frame. Since there are 525 lines that make up a complete frame, or $\frac{1}{30}$ of a second, scanning every other line yields $262\frac{1}{2}$ lines scanned per field, or $\frac{1}{60}$ of a second (Figure 3.4). Two fields of $262\frac{1}{2}$ lines each combine to make 525 lines, or one complete frame ($2 \times \frac{1}{60}$ of a second $= \frac{2}{60}$ or $\frac{1}{30}$ of a second) (Figure 3.5). The process is the same in PAL and SECAM, taking into consideration their line and frame rates.

Interlace Scanning

The process of this field-by-field scanning is known as *interlace scanning* because the lines in each field interlace with the alternate lines of the other field. There are two fields for each frame. Because the images are appearing at the rate of $\frac{1}{60}$ of a second, the eye does not see the interval between the two fields. Therefore, continuous motion is perceived.

An interesting experiment to better understand the concept of interlace scanning is to follow a similar scanning pattern as the electron beam would on a frame of video. Look at the paragraph below and first read just the bolded odd lines. Then go back to the top of the paragraph and read the unbolded even lines. Notice the way the eyes retrace from the end of a line back to the left margin to begin scanning the next odd line. At the end of the paragraph, the eyes retrace from the last line back to the top again to read or scan the even lines. This is what the electron beam does during its blanking periods.

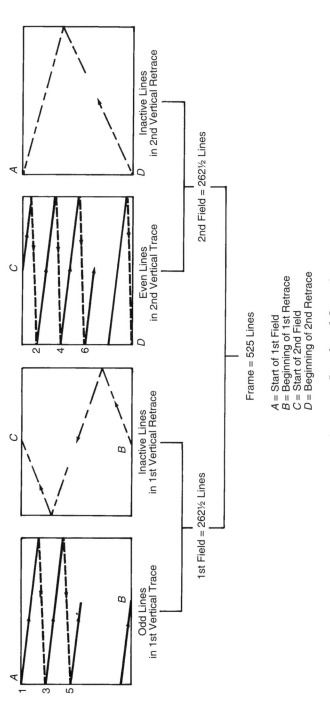

Figure 3.4 Interlaced Scanning

A = Start of 1st Field
B = Beginning of 1st Retrace
C = Start of 2nd Field
D = Beginning of 2nd Retrace

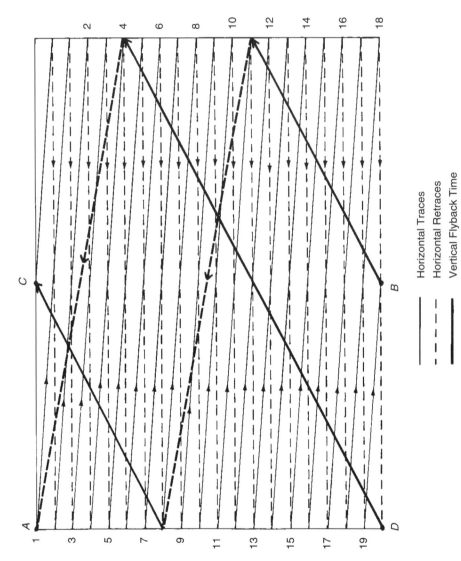

Figure 3.5 Interlaced Frame

Horizontal Traces
Horizontal Retraces
Vertical Flyback Time

A television image is created through
Interlace scanning. Interlace scanning
is the process of scanning every other
line from top to bottom. The beam
first scans the odd lines top to bottom,
and then it scans the even lines top to bottom.
Each scan from top to bottom
is a field. It is the combination of the
two successive fields that make up an
entire frame of a video image.

It is not until both sets (or fields) of odd lines and even lines are interlaced together that the full meaning of the paragraph (or full-frame image) becomes clear. This holds true especially with electronic graphics. When viewing only one field, the letters look ragged and uneven. Only when viewing a complete interlaced frame do the letters look smooth and even.

Black and White Specifications

Dividing the video image into two fields, each with $262\frac{1}{2}$ lines, provides an advantage when broadcasting a video signal. Since there is much less information in $262\frac{1}{2}$ lines than there is in 525 lines, the video signal does not require as much bandwidth or spectrum space for transmission.

For black and white video images, the original NTSC standards were as follows:

- 525 lines per frame
- 480 lines per frame of active video
- 30 frames per second
- 15,750 lines per second (line frequency)
- $262\frac{1}{2}$ lines per field
- 2 fields per frame
- 60 fields per second

- Horizontal blanking before each line
- Vertical blanking between successive fields

These specifications are different when color is added to the video signal. Color specifications will be covered in Chapter 6.

CHAPTER 4

Synchronizing the Analog Signal

Video images are generated from a source, such as a camera or computer, and viewed on a source, such as a monitor. In order for the viewed image to be seen in exactly the same way and the same time frame as the generated or original image, there has to be a method for synchronizing the elements of the image. Synchronizing an image is a critical part of the analog video process.

Synchronizing Generators

A *synchronizing generator*, or *sync generator* as it is called, is the heart of the analog video system. The sync generator creates a series of pulses that drive all the different equipment in the entire video facility, from cameras to monitors. When viewing analog signals, the synchronizing pulses also drive the monitors.

The heart of the sync generator is an oscillator that puts out a signal called the *color subcarrier*. The frequency of the color subcarrier is 3,579,545 cycles per second, rounded off and more commonly referred to as 3.58. Starting with this basic signal, the sync generator, through a process of electronic multiplication and division, outputs other frequencies in order to create the other pulses that are necessary for driving video equipment. These pulses include horizontal and vertical synchronizing pulses, horizontal and vertical drive pulses, horizontal and vertical blanking, and equalizing pulses (Figure 4.1).

These pulses are often combined so that one signal will contain multiple synchronizing components. Combination signals are

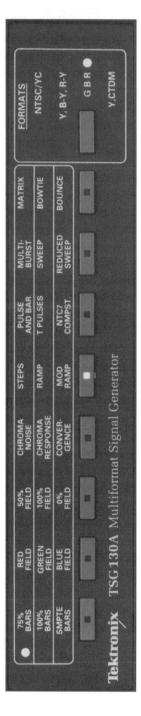

Figure 4.1 Sync Generator

referred to as *composite signals*. Terms such as *composite blanking* and *composite video* refer to such signals.

Synchronizing Pulses

The sync generator puts out both *horizontal* and *vertical synchronizing pulses*. These synchronizing pulses ensure that all of the equipment within the system is in time or synchronized with each other. Horizontal and vertical synchronizing pulses are part of the composite signal, so they can be easily fed to any piece of equipment that requires a sync reference signal.

Horizontal synchronizing pulses appear at the beginning of each line of video. They assure that monitors and receivers are in synchronization on a line-by-line basis with the information that the camera is creating. Vertical synchronizing pulses appear during the vertical interval, which will be discussed later in this chapter. These pulses assure that the retrace is taking place properly, so that the gun is in its proper position for painting the beginning of the next field.

The composite sync signal ensures that each piece of equipment is operating within the system on a line-by-line, field-by-field basis. If equipment is not synchronized, switching between images can cause the image in the monitor to lose stability. Dissolves and special effects can change color or shift position. Character generators or computer-generated images might appear in a different position in the image from where they were originally placed.

Drive Pulses

Horizontal and *vertical drive pulses* are used for driving the camera and are never broadcast. These pulses trigger circuits in the camera called *sawtooth waveform generators*. The name "sawtooth waveform" refers to the shape of its signal, which looks like the serrations on the edge of a wood saw (Figure 4.2). Both the horizontal and vertical circuits are driven by the same sawtooth waveform.

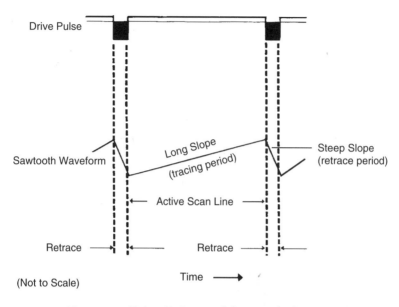

Figure 4.2 Drive Pulses and Sawtooth Current

In *horizontal deflection circuits*, the long slope on the sawtooth wave-form drives the scanning electron beam horizontally across the target face of the pickup tube. In *vertical deflection circuits*, the long slope moves the beam vertically from one scanning line to the next. In both horizontal and vertical deflection circuits, the shorter and steeper slope of the sawtooth waveform causes the beam to retrace. In horizontal deflection circuits, the beam moves back to start scanning another line. In vertical deflection circuits, the beam moves back to begin scanning another field.

Blanking Pulses

Horizontal and *vertical blanking pulses* cause the electron beam in a video camera to go into blanking. In other words, they cause the electron beam to shut off during the retrace period at the end of each line and the retrace period at the end of each field. Blanking pulses, like horizontal and vertical drive pulses, are fed to cameras.

However, unlike drive pulses, the blanking pulses are broadcast as part of the overall video signal.

Horizontal Blanking

Horizontal retrace occurs during the *horizontal blanking* period. The horizontal blanking period can be viewed on a waveform monitor, which displays an electronic representation of the visual image (Figure 4.3, *A*). (The waveform monitor is discussed in detail in Chapter 8.) Several critical synchronizing signals occur during this horizontal blanking period. These signals appear in the following order: the front porch, the horizontal synchronizing pulse, the breezeway, and color burst reference. (See definitions of these terms below.) The breezeway and color burst reference occur during the period of time referred to as the back porch (Figure 4.3, *B*).

The *front porch* is the period of time that begins at the end of active video. It initiates the retrace and is the beginning of the synchronizing period of time. A single scan line is defined as starting at the front porch and ending with active video before the next front porch begins.

Following the front porch is the *horizontal synchronizing pulse*. This pulse synchronizes the receiver with the originating source that created the image. Following the horizontal synchronizing pulse is the area known as the *back porch*. With the advent of color, the *color burst signal* was inserted in the back porch. The area between horizontal sync and color burst on the back porch is called the *breezeway*. Following the end of the back porch, the active video scanning portion of the line begins.

Vertical Blanking

Vertical blanking is somewhat more complex. During the vertical blanking period, there are *pre-* and *post-equalizing pulses* and *vertical sync pulses*, as well as several lines of blanked video. These are full lines of video on which there is no active picture. The vertical blanking period can also be seen on a waveform monitor (Figure 4.4).

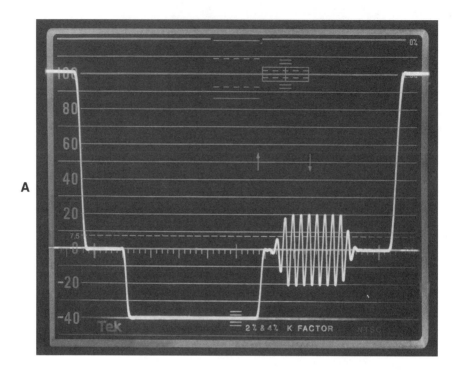

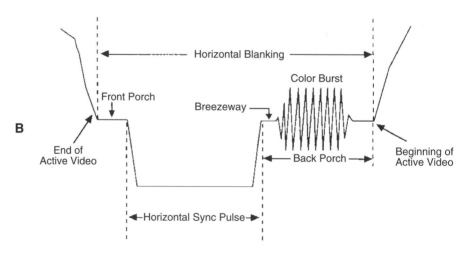

Figure 4.3 **A** and **B**, Horizontal Blanking Interval

Vertical Synchronizing Pulses

Vertical synchronizing pulses, which are part of the broadcast signal, are used to drive the electron beam back to the beginning of the next field so that the horizontal trace can be initiated. There are six vertical synchronizing pulses that occur between fields to initiate this process. Vertical synchronizing pulses only occur between fields.

Equalizing Pulses

During the vertical blanking interval, the sync generator puts out *equalizing pulses*. Equalizing pulses occur both before and after the vertical sync signal. The equalizing pulses that occur before the vertical sync are called *pre-equalizing pulses*. Those that occur after vertical sync are called *post-equalizing pulses*. Equalizing pulses in video assure continued synchronization during vertical retrace as well as proper interlace of the odd and even fields (Figure 4.4).

Lines 1 through 9 in each field actually consist of pre-equalizing pulses, vertical sync pulses, and post-equalizing pulses. The 6 pre-equalizing pulses break up the first 3 lines of a field into 6 half-lines. The next 3 lines consist of 6 vertical sync pulses. Lines 7, 8, and 9 are separated by post-equalizing pulses.

Depending on whether it is the odd or even field, there will be 6 post-equalizing pulses, but either 5 or 6 half-lines. In the even field, there are only 5 half-lines. The first half-line of inactive video is called line 9. In the odd field, there are 6 post-equalizing pulses and 6 half-lines, so that the first full line of inactive video is called line 10.

There are other ways of defining fields. Each field consists of $262\frac{1}{2}$ lines. The odd field begins with a whole line of active video on line 21 and ends with a half-line of video. The even field is defined as starting active video with a half-line on line 20 and ending with a whole line of video. In either case, each field is handled individually, and line counting is done within each field.

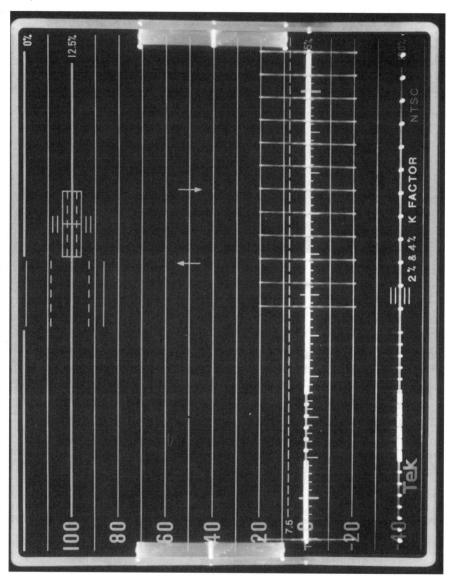

A

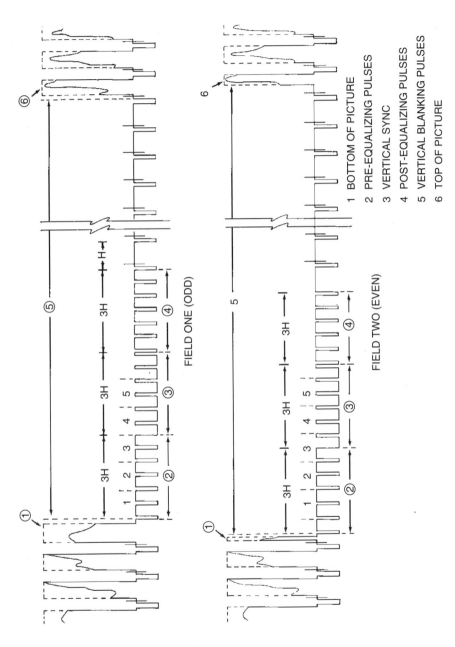

1 BOTTOM OF PICTURE
2 PRE-EQUALIZING PULSES
3 VERTICAL SYNC
4 POST-EQUALIZING PULSES
5 VERTICAL BLANKING PULSES
6 TOP OF PICTURE

FIELD ONE (ODD)

FIELD TWO (EVEN)

Figure 4.4 (continued) **A** and **B**, Vertical Interval

It is the equalizing pulses that allow the system to distinguish the odd from the even field and therefore interlace the two proper fields together to create one frame. If the fields were not properly inter-laced, it would be possible to be a field off in the interlace process.

Color Subcarrier

With the advent of color television, a new signal was introduced to carry the color information. This signal, known as the *color subcar-rier*, became the most important signal of the sync generator. Most sync generators combine color subcarrier with horizontal sync, vertical sync, blanking, and a black video signal to produce a com-posite signal called *black burst* or *color black*. The color subcarrier signal, or any of the synchronizing or blanking pulses, can be taken as a separate output from a sync generator. However, the combin-ation of sync pulses in a black burst signal is much more useful.

The frequency of the color subcarrier is 3,579,545 cycles per second. This frequency must be maintained within plus or minus 10 cycles per second. If this frequency changes, the rate of change cannot be greater than one cycle per second every second. The exactness of this specification has to do with the sensitivity of the human eye to changes in color. As this color subcarrier signal is the reference for color information, any change in the frequency would cause a shift in the color balance. The color subcarrier is also used as the main reference signal for the entire video signal. If the color sub-carrier is incorrect, then all the signals in the television system will be affected.

Cross Pulse

On a professional video monitor, the image can be shifted horizon-tally to make the horizontal blanking period visible. The image can also be shifted vertically to make the vertical blanking interval visible (Figure 4.5, *A*). When the image is shifted both horizontally and vertically at the same time, the display is known as a *cross pulse* or *pulse cross* display. A cross pulse display is a visual image of

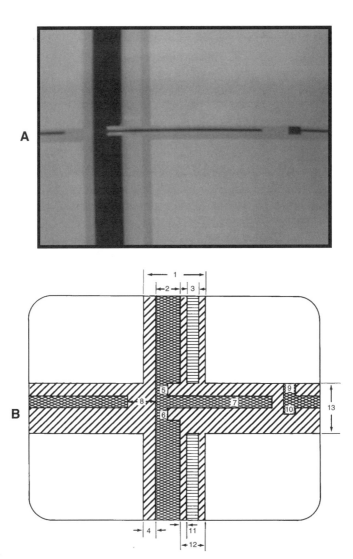

1. Horizontal Blanking
2. Horizontal Sync
3. Color Burst (if present)
4. Front Porch
5. Odd and Even Leading Equalizing Pulses
6. Odd and Even Trailing Equalizing Pulses
7. Odd Vertical sync

8. Vertical Serrations
9. Odd and even Leading Equalizing Pulses
10. Odd and Even trailing equalizing Pulses
11. Breezeway
12. Back Porch
13. Vertical Blanking

Figure 4.5 A and **B,** Cross Pulse Display

what is represented electronically on a waveform monitor. This display shows several of the signals created in the sync generator (Figure 4.5, *B*).

Other Signal Outputs

There are several other outputs from the synchronizing generator that are used for testing or other purposes. These *test signal outputs* are not so much used for driving the system as they are for checking it, or checking the synchronizing generator itself.

Quite often, test signal outputs and black burst or color subcarrier appear at the front of the sync generator for ease of access, though they are also available at the back of the sync generator. Horizontal and vertical drive pulses may be available at the rear of the sync generator, as they are not used for testing purposes or to drive any other piece of equipment other than a tube camera (Figure 4.6). Test signals that are available from a sync generator are discussed in Chapter 21.

Vertical Interval Signals

The NTSC analog video image is 525 lines, 480 of which represent picture information, referred to as active video. The remaining lines in the vertical interval are used for synchronizing information. Test signals are inserted in the vertical interval as well. While not part of the active video, they are a valuable part of the composite signal.

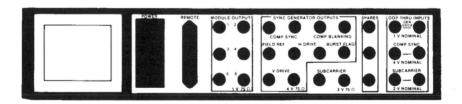

Figure 4.6 Rear View of Sync Generator

These signals are usually created by devices connected to one or more of the outputs of a sync generator. These extra signals can then be inserted in the vertical interval. These signals may include vertical interval test signals, vertical interval reference signals, closed captioning, teletext, commercial insertion data, and satellite data.

In the case of the *vertical interval test signals*, or *VITS*, a test signal generator can create one-line representations of several test signals. These one-line test signals are inserted in one of the unused video lines in the vertical interval. The VITS can be displayed on an oscilloscope. This test signal provides a constant reference with respect to the active video contained within the frame.

The *vertical interval reference signal*, or *VIRS*, was developed to maintain color fidelity. Small differences in color synchronization can occur when signals are switched between pieces of equipment. The VIRS provides a constant color reference for the monitor or receiver. Without the VIRS, the color balance of the image may change.

Closed captioning was originally developed so the hearing impaired could watch a program and understand the dialogue. In closed captioning, a special receiver takes the information from the vertical interval and decodes it into subtitles in the active video. Closed captioning may also be used in environments where the audio may not be appropriate or desired. Technically, since closed captioning appears on line 21, which is active video, the data is not truly in the vertical interval.

Teletext can be used for broadcasting completely separate information unrelated to program content. An example of this is seen on many cable news stations. While the camera may be covering a news story or pointing to an anchor, the ticker tape of information below the image is an ongoing feed of text.

Commercial insertion data can be used to automatically initiate the playback of a commercial. This can eliminate the possibility of operator error. The data are designed to trigger the playback of the required material at the appropriate time, as well as for verification that the commerical was broadcast as ordered.

Satellite data contain information about the satellite being used, the specific channel or transponder on the satellite, and the frequencies used for the audio signals.

The blanking portions of the video signal, both horizontal and vertical, carry critical information. In addition to synchronizing, the blanking periods are used to carry other data that enhance the quality and usefulness of the video signal.

CHAPTER 5

The Transmitted Signal

Television transmission is the process of sending the video, audio, and synchronizing signals from a transmitting facility to a receiver. In trying to get a package from one city to another, one would arrange for a truck, train or airplane to be the carrier of that package to its destination. What happens in radio and television is similar in that specific frequencies are designated as the carriers for radio and television signals. The signal that carries the information is directed out into the air so that receivers tuned to the frequency of the carrier can pick up the signal. Once it picks up the signal, the receiver can extract the information from the carrier.

Modulating the Signal

To put this information on the carrier, a process called *modulation* is used. To modulate means to make a change. In music, changing key is referred to as modulating to a different key. The melody and harmony of the song sound the same, but the key or pitch is lower or higher. In broadcasting, making this change to the carrier is called *modulating* the carrier.

There are two ways to modulate a carrier. One way is to change the height or amplitude of signals that are imposed on the carrier. The other way is to impose signals on the carrier that vary in speed or frequency. Think of the carrier wave as being the ride to the destination and the modulation of the carrier as the passenger. The *amplitude change* or *modulation* is referred to as *AM*, and the *frequency modulation* is referred to as *FM* (Figure 5.1). In television broadcasting, the video image is transmitted by amplitude

Unmodulated Carrier

Modulated Carrier

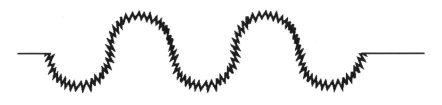

Amplitude Modulation (AM)

Frequency Modulation (FM)

Figure 5.1

modulation of the carrier. The audio portion of the signal is transmitted by frequency modulation of the carrier.

Originally, light was converted into varying voltages in the camera. Now these voltage variations are used to make changes in amplitude on the carrier wave. These changes in amplitude are proportional to the original picture voltage which came from the light on the face of the target.

For a monitor or receiver to show the original image, it must first receive the carrier. When a receiver is tuned to a specific channel, it becomes sensitive to the frequency of that carrier wave. The receiver, through the process of *demodulation*, takes the varying amplitude changes off the carrier and converts that information back to varying voltages proportional to the amplitude changes on the carrier.

Now, the reverse process of what happened in the camera takes place. The varying voltage levels are converted to light by the beam of electrons scanning the phosphors on the inside face of the receiver tube. This brings the process full circle back to the varying light levels that originally made up the picture on the face of the target or the CCD.

In addition to the main video carrier, there are two other carriers that send out information about the audio and the color portion of the signal. These three modulated carriers, one for video, one for color, and one for audio, make up the total composite signal.

Frequency Spectrum

In nature, the spectrum of frequencies ranges from zero to infinity. The spectrum is referred to in terms of *cycles per second*, or *hertz* *(Hz)*, named in honor of the scientist, Heinrich Hertz, who did many early experiments with magnetism and electricity.

Three of the five senses human beings experience, hearing, seeing, and touch, are sensitive to the frequency spectrum. For example, the ear is capable of hearing between 20 and 20,000 Hz, or 20 kHz (kilohertz). Human beings are generally unable to hear sounds above 20 kHz. At extremely high frequencies, our eyes become sensitive to a certain portion of the spectrum and are able to see light and color. Light with frequencies between 432 trillion hertz and 732 trillion hertz become visible. Frequencies below 432 trillion hertz are called *infrared*. Infrared frequencies can be felt as heat, but cannot be seen by the human eye. Frequencies above 732 trillion hertz are called *ultraviolet*. Skin exposed to ultraviolet light can become damaged, as can one's eyesight (Figure 5.2). Only a small portion of the total spectrum is directly perceptible to human sensation without the aid of tools.

Analog and Digital Broadcasting

The frequency spectrum is divided into sections, some of which have been given names. They include the following: Low Frequency (LF), Intermediate Frequency (IF), Radio Frequency (RF), Very High Frequency (VHF), and Ultra High Frequency (UHF). Portions of the VHF and UHF spectrum space have been allocated for use in analog television broadcasting. Television channels between 1 and 13 are in the VHF or Very High Frequency range. Channels 14 through channel 59 are in the UHF or Ultra High Frequency range. Channel 1 is not used, only channels 2 through 59 (Figure 5.3).

Certain analog television channels have a greater separation in the spectrum between the assigned carrier frequency for one channel and another. For example, in a city where there is a channel 2, there cannot be a channel 3, because the separation between these two channels is too narrow and the signals would interfere with each other. However, in a city where there is a channel 4, there can also be a channel 5. This is because the separation in the spectrum between these two channels allows enough room for each to transmit without interference from the other.

In the conversion from analog to digital broadcasting, new spectrum allocations are being made for the digital channels. A digital

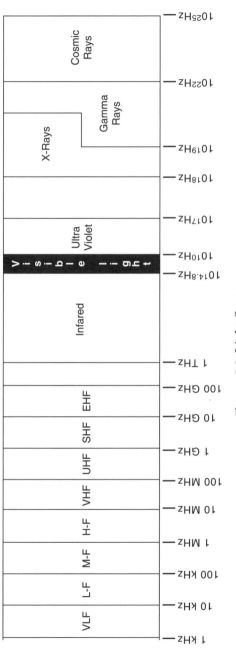

Figure 5.2 Light Spectrum

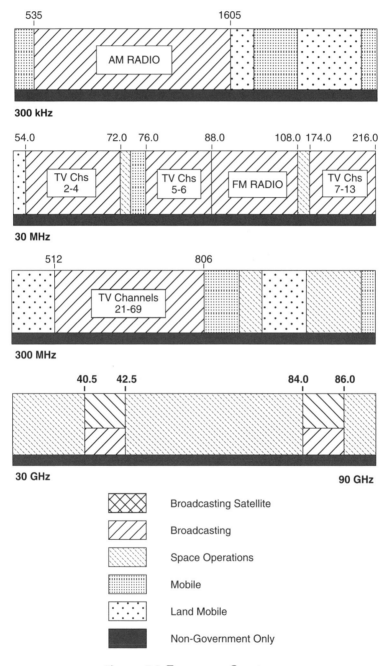

Figure 5.3 Frequency Spectrum

signal comprised of zeros and ones, thanks to compression techniques, requires considerably less spectrum space for broadcasting than analog waves. Spectrum space can be conserved by converting to an all-digital environment. As digital broadcasting becomes the standard, eventually the analog frequency allocations for television broadcasting will be reassigned for other uses.

With the advent of cable, more channels have become available because the cable signal does not take up spectrum space. The cable signal is sent by wire so the channels can be right next to each other without causing interference.

Bandwidth

When the television system was originally created, a carrier frequency was assigned for each channel. It was also decided that 6 MHz (megahertz) of *bandwidth* or spectrum space would be made available for the transmission of television signals on the carrier for each particular station. A signal has an upper and a lower half, referred to as the upper and lower side bands. The 6 MHz of bandwidth in television broadcasting uses the upper side band only for transmission. If both upper and lower side bands were used, they would take up 12 MHz of space. The lower side band is vestigial because it is not used and is filtered off before transmission. All the information necessary for the re-creation of the television signal is contained in the upper side band.

This limitation of 6 MHz of bandwidth for a television signal is one of the reasons the field process, or interlaced scanning process, was developed. To transmit all 525 lines of information at once would take far more bandwidth than the 6 MHz allocated for each television station. Consequently it was decided, not only to minimize flicker, but also for the conservation of spectrum space, to transmit only one field at a time.

For example, channel 2 was given between 54 and 60 MHz as the 6 MHz bandwidth spread allowed for transmission. In television, the visual carrier is placed $1\frac{1}{4}$-MHz above the low end of the allowable spectrum. Thus channel 2's assigned carrier is 55.25 MHz.

The *audio carrier*, which is separate from the video, is always $4\frac{1}{2}$-MHz above the assigned carrier frequency for video. For channel 2, this means the audio carrier is 59.75 MHz, allowing $\frac{1}{4}$ MHz of room between the audio carrier and the upper end of the allowed spectrum space (Figure 5.4). The third carrier in the television signal is the *color subcarrier*, which will be discussed in detail in the following chapter.

When a broadcast channel is selected on a television set, the receiver becomes sensitive to the particular carrier frequency in the spectrum that is assigned to that channel. The television set then receives that carrier and the information that is on it. It strips off the carrier frequency as unnecessary and demodulates the information that was contained on the carrier, and thus recreates the original television image.

Satellites

Television signals are referred to as *line of sight signals* because they do not bend with the curve of the earth. They penetrate through the atmosphere and continue into space. Because of this, getting television reception beyond 80 miles or so becomes difficult, if not impossible. Since height plays such a major factor in sending and receiving television signals, mountain tops and high antennas are used to provide as much range as possible from the earth. It was impractical to get any greater range than this until the development of satellite communications.

Satellites operate on the principle of rebound, bouncing a signal from one place to another. The concept is similar to the game of pool, where a ball is purposely banked off of one side of the table to go into a hole on the other. Satellites launched from the earth are put into orbit around the equator at an altitude of 22,300 miles. This gives them a very high point from which to bounce signals to the

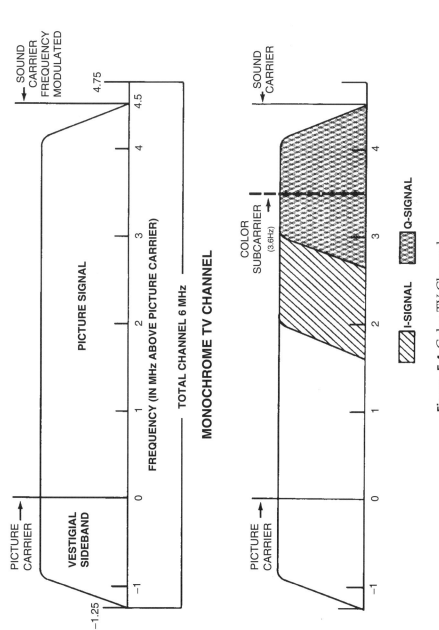

Figure 5.4 Color TV Channel

earth. It allows greater geographic coverage and overcomes the problem of *the curve of the horizon*. When satellites are placed in orbit, they are set in motion to move at the same speed as the rotation of the earth. These factors make the satellite *geosynchronous*, or stationary, above the earth.

A satellite will appear to stay in a fixed position in the sky for the duration of its life span, which has been about ten years. At this point, solar cells begin to show their age, and satellites run out of the fuel necessary to make orbital adjustments during their lifetime. Methods have been developed for refurbishing the satellites, thus increasing their life and saving the cost of a new satellite and the cost of placing it in orbit.

Satellites are placed into orbit at specific degree points around the equator. The orbital space along the equatorial arc is assigned by international agreement, similar to the spectrum space in broadcast frequencies. The North American continent, including the U.S., Canada, and Mexico, has from approximately 67° to 143° west longitude. The early satellites were placed 4° apart around the equator, and each satellite had as many as 12 *transponders*, or channels of communication, available. With improvements in the technology of both the antennas and the electronics, spacing has been reduced to 1° in the equatorial arc. The new satellites have as many as 48 transponders available and that amount continues to increase steadily.

Uplink and Downlink

Standards conversion, the process of converting television signals from one standard to another, can be achieved via satellite. The broadcaster or *uplink* facility sends up one standard of television signal and the receiving end, or *downlink* facility, picks up or records the signal in the standard of its choice. In fact, a great deal of program distribution is achieved via satellite. Programs are sent up on a satellite for receiving stations to record. On occasion, when long-distance transmission is required, two satellites may be used in what is called a *double hop*.

For example, in a double hop from Los Angeles to Paris, the signal would be transmitted to a satellite over North America and received at a downlink facility perhaps in New York City or Montreal. This facility would then uplink the signal to a satellite over the Atlantic Ocean. The signal would then be received at a downlink facility in Paris.

The area of the earth that the satellite signal covers is known as the *footprint*. The size of the footprint can be as large or as confined as the operator of the satellite wishes. For general television purposes in the continental United States, the footprint covers the entire country. In Europe, footprints can be confined to a single country or allowed to cover the entire continent (Figure 5.5).

In setting the antenna of a satellite dish for either an up or downlink, there are three positions to align. The first is the elevation or angle above the earth at which the antenna is set. The second is the degree or compass heading toward which the antenna is pointing. The third is the polarity, or horizontal or vertical alignment, of the antenna. These three specifications allow the antenna to be pointed at an exact place in the sky to find the signal. The exactness of these alignments is critical.

If any of these measurements are incorrect, it is possible that the signal will be received by a satellite or transponder assigned to a different uplink facility. The result is two images superimposed on each other at the downlink facilities assigned to receive the images. This is referred to as *double illumination*. Two signals received by the same transponder on the same satellite at the same time renders both images useless. If the satellite dish is misaligned for the downlink or reception, the quality of the image that is received will be compromised.

The size of the parabolic dish that receives or transmits a signal to a satellite also plays a factor in the ability to discriminate between the various satellites and transponders. For transmission purposes, the law requires a minimum dish size of nine meters in diameter. This requirement is to assure the transmit-

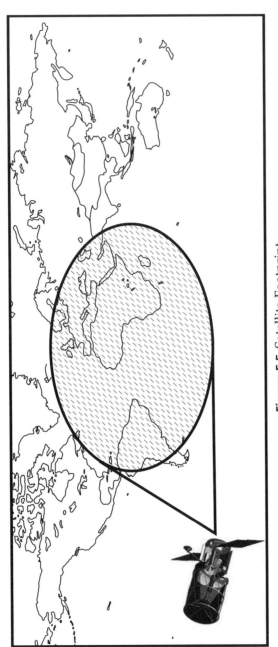

Figure 5.5 Satellite Footprint

ted signal reaches its specific target, or satellite. The receiver dish can be any size, but again, the larger the dish, the better the reception.

Satellite signals travel at the speed of light. The actual distance traveled is almost 45,000 miles round trip. Because of this distance, there is a delay of about a quarter of a second from transmission to reception.

CHAPTER 6
Color Video

Color, like sound, is based on frequencies. Each color has its own specific frequency in the visible spectrum and its own specific wavelength. Each color is defined scientifically by its frequency or its wavelength. Wavelength is related to frequency in that the higher the frequency, the shorter the physical length of the wave. Color frequencies are extremely high in the spectrum, and therefore are easier to notate by wavelength, rather than frequency (cycles per second or hertz). Wavelengths of light are measured in nanometers, or billionths of a meter.

Additive and Subtractive

There are two ways that color is perceived. First, by adding the frequencies of light together, which is referred to as *additive*. Any light-emitting system, such as a television monitor, is additive. In an additive environment, the combination of all the primary colors yields white light. Sunlight, which is a combination of all the colors, is additive.

Conversely, all solid objects, including print media, do not emit light and are perceived through a *subtractive* process. That is, the objects absorb every color frequency that the object is *not*. All colors are subtracted except the ones seen, which are reflected. Therefore, the color of an object is the light reflected by it. In a subtractive color system, all the colors added together yield black. This is because all the frequencies are absorbed by the object and none are reflected.

Primary and Secondary Colors

In any color system, certain colors are referred to as *primary*. The definition of a primary color is that it cannot be created through a combination of any of the other primary colors. For example, in a red, green, and blue color system (RGB), red cannot be created by combining blue and green, green cannot be created by combining red and blue, and blue cannot be created by combining red and green. When defining a color system, any set of colors can be used as the primaries. A primary color system can include more than three primary colors. Again, the only rule that must be adhered to is that the combination of any two of the primary colors cannot create one of the other primaries.

The basic color system in television is a three primary color additive system. The primary colors in television are red, green, and blue (RGB). Combing two primary colors creates a *secondary* color. Combining secondary colors creates a *tertiary* color. In the color television system, there are three secondary colors, yellow, cyan, and magenta, which are each combinations of two primary colors. Yellow is the combination of red and green, cyan is the combination of green and blue, and magenta is a combination of red and blue (Figure 6.1).

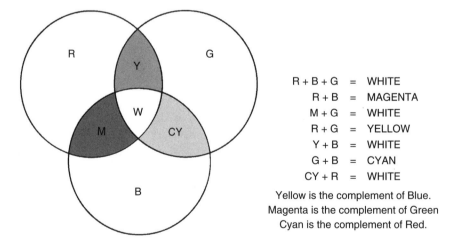

$$R + B + G = \text{WHITE}$$
$$R + B = \text{MAGENTA}$$
$$M + G = \text{WHITE}$$
$$R + G = \text{YELLOW}$$
$$Y + B = \text{WHITE}$$
$$G + B = \text{CYAN}$$
$$CY + R = \text{WHITE}$$

Yellow is the complement of Blue.
Magenta is the complement of Green
Cyan is the complement of Red.

Figure 6.1 Primary and Secondary Colors

The Color System

The first NTSC television systems that were developed were black and white, or monochrome. NTSC television transmission was created around 6 MHz of spectrum space for transmission of the black and white picture and audio signal.

The development of NTSC color posed a problem because monochrome television system was already in place. Adding color information to the monochrome signal would be an easy enough solution, but doing that would take up twice the amount of spectrum space. This wasn't possible given the system currently in place. Also, this color system would not be compatible with the existing black and white system. The trick to adding color onto the existing black and white carrier would be to add it within the 6 MHz of bandwidth, thus maintaining compatibility.

As with many challenges in television, part of the solution is a game of numbers. By simply working with the mathematics and changing some of the numbers, changes in the system can be made without changing its basic structure. The PAL and SECAM systems were developed following the NTSC color system.

Harmonics

Harmonics and octaves play an important role in the process of creating color video. An *octave* is a doubling of a frequency. For example, in music, the tuning note "A" lies at 440 hertz. To hear another "A" an octave above this, the frequency would be doubled to 880 hertz. An octave above 1,000 hertz would be 2,000 hertz. An octave above 2,000 would be 4,000; an octave above 4,000 would be 8,000; and so on.

Harmonics, on the other hand, are frequencies that change by adding the initial frequency or fundamental tone to itself again, rather than doubling the frequency. For example, if the first harmonic or fundamental tone is 1,000 hertz, the second harmonic would be 2,000 hertz, the third harmonic 3,000, the fourth harmonic 4,000, and so on.

The NTSC monochrome television *line frequency* was 15,750 hertz. Harmonics of that number can be found by adding 15,750 hertz to itself. The second harmonic would be 31,500 hertz, the third 47,250 hertz, and so on. What was discovered in television was that the video information modulated on the carrier frequency seemed to be grouping itself around the harmonics of the line frequency. That left places on the carrier where little or no information was being carried.

These spaces in the carrier were discovered to be mathematically at the odd harmonics of half of the line frequency (Figure 6.2). Half of the line frequency was 7,875 lines per second. If that is the first harmonic, then the third harmonic would be 3 times 7,875, or 23,625. The fifth harmonic would be 5 times 7,875, or 39,375, and so on up the scale into the megahertz range.

Examining the carrier revealed that space was available at these frequencies. Other video information could be inserted in these spaces without causing any interference with the existing information being broadcast. Using these spaces for color information meant that the existing black and white system and the new color system could be compatible.

NTSC Color Transmission

In order to transmit the color portion of the NTSC signal, an additional carrier frequency was needed. The idea was to make that new carrier frequency as high as possible because higher frequency signals cause less interference and would result in fewer problems in the existing black and white system. So the 455th harmonic of half the line frequency was set as the *color subcarrier frequency*. It is called a subcarrier because it is an additional carrier of information within the main carrier.

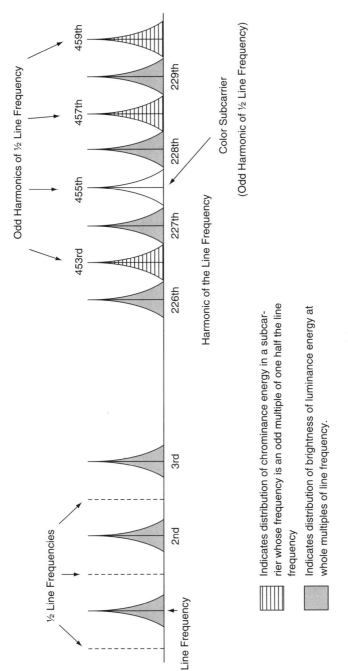

Figure 6.2 Odd Harmonics

This in itself caused another problem. All audio carriers were set at 4.5 MHz above the video carrier for all television stations. Whatever the frequency of the video carrier, television sets were made so that they would detect the audio carrier at 4.5 MHz above that. It was discovered that the new color subcarrier caused a *beat frequency*, or interference, to occur with the audio carrier somewhere in the order of 900 kilohertz. This was visible as wavy black and white lines going through the picture. The problem then became how to eliminate that beat frequency and its visible interference.

Since all television sets looked for the audio carrier at 4.5 MHz above the visual carrier, the audio carrier could not be changed. At the same time, the color subcarrier was derived mathematically from an already existing line frequency and could not be changed arbitrarily.

It was discovered that by slowing the existing line frequency of 15,750 lines per second to approximately 15,734 lines per second, the 455th harmonic of half of that would be a color subcarrier frequency that would not interfere with the audio carrier in a way that was visible. This color subcarrier fits properly in one of the spaces created by harmonics of the line frequency.

At the same time, this new line frequency, which was essentially 16 lines slower than the existing black and white system, was still compatible with existing television sets. Television equipment was designed to work within a range of approximately 1% variation in line frequency. One percent of 15,750 is approximately 157 lines. As the new line frequency was only slowed down by approximately 16 lines, it was within $\frac{1}{10}$ of 1% of the existing line frequency.

NTSC Color Frame Rate

Black and white television sets of that time could handle this change and not display any interference. The slightly slower line frequency produced a new frame rate of 29.97 frames per second. This means that it took slightly longer than one second to complete scanning a full 30 frames. With color television, the 29.97 frame rate, or 59.94 field rate, does not lock with 60 cycle current, or AC (alternating current). Consequently, synchronizing references needed to change. Therefore, analog television systems were referenced to the color subcarrier.

However, the information needed for all three colors (the red, green, and blue signals) would not fit in the available spaces on the carrier. A system of *encoding* was needed in order to compact all of this information onto the color subcarrier signal.

The process of encoding the red, green, and blue information is based on mathematics and, in this case, plane geometry. In plane geometry, the Pythagorean theorem states that the sum of the squares of the sides of a right triangle is equal to the square of the third side. That means that if the measurements of two sides of a right triangle are known, the third side can be calculated. Using the Pythagorean theorem, if the strength of two of the colors is known, the third can be calculated. Red and blue became the measured signals, and green the derived or calculated value.

Vectors

Color video is represented as vectors. A *vector* is a mathematical representation of a force in a particular direction. The length of a vector represents the amount of force, and the direction of the vector is where the vector is pointed with respect to a fixed reference, rather like a compass. The piece of equipment used to view and measure these vectors is called a *vectorscope* (Figure 6.3). Like the waveform monitor, the vectorscope displays an electronic representation of the visual image. (The vectorscope is discussed in more detail in Chapter 9.) In television, the direction of the vector dictates a specific color, and the length represents the amount of that color.

In a three-chip color video camera, there is one chip for each of the three primary colors. The voltage output from each of these chips is the length of the vector. The direction of the vector is specified as the number of degrees away from a reference point. In color

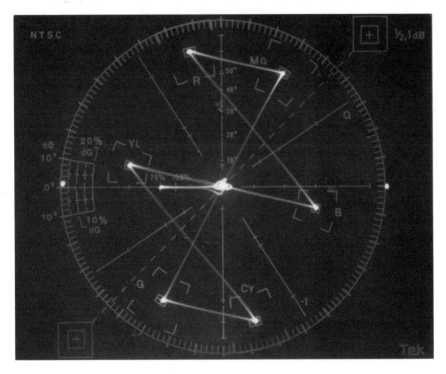

Figure 6.3 Color Bars on Vectorscope

television, the reference point is along the horizontal axis that points to the left, or nine o'clock, on a vectorscope. This reference point is defined as zero degrees.

Everything goes around the circle from that point, and from there the various colors are defined. For example, red is defined as being 76.5° clockwise from that reference point. Blue is 192° clockwise, and green is just a little less than 300° (Figure 6.3).

Color Burst

The reference point mentioned above is the part of the video signal known as *color burst*. Color burst is a burst or portion of just the *color subcarrier*. It is not modulated and does not contain any of the other color information.

The burst appears on the waveform monitor as a series of cycles during the back porch or the horizontal blanking period (see Figure 4.3). It appears on the vectorscope as the line going toward the left, or toward nine o'clock, from the center of the circle (Figure 6.3). It also appears on the video monitor in the pulse cross display as a yellow-green bar going down the screen in the horizontal blanking period (see Figure 4.5).

Note that the burst, which is made up of 8 to 11 cycles of subcarrier, has an amplitude and direction and thus actually has a color. The burst is used as the reference for a receiver to decode the color information that is contained in each line of the incoming video signal.

Chrominance and Luminance

Color is defined by three measurements: (1) *chrominance*, the amount of color information; (2) *luminance*, the amount of white light that is mixed with the color information; and (3) *hue*, the particular color pigment.

The combination of color and light, or chrominance and luminance, produces *saturation*. Saturation is the ratio between how much color and how much light there is in the signal (Figure 6.4). If more white light is added to a color, it becomes desaturated. If the white light is removed, the color becomes more saturated. Consider the difference between red and pink. Pink is the same hue as red, except it has more white light in it, which desaturates it. The method used to add more color in an additive system is to add proportionate amounts of the other two primaries, as the combination of all three is white.

In color television, the length of the vector represents the saturation and the direction of that vector represents the hue. To be able to replicate colors correctly in a television system, there has to be

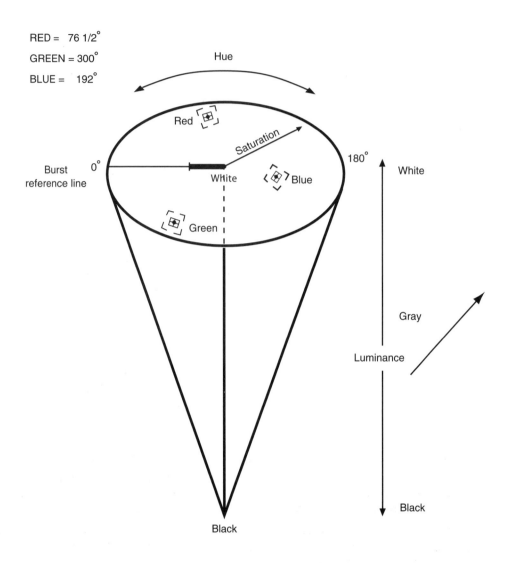

LUMINANCE = Brightness (Black to White)

HUE = Color (Red, Blue, Green, etc.)

SATURATION = Depth of Color (Pink as compared to Red)

Figure 6.4 Color Vector Cone

an exact definition of the chrominance to luminance ratio for each color, as well as the direction of the vector in relation to the reference color burst. The colors are described in degrees. The saturation or chrominance to luminance ratio in television is given in percentages. Those percentages and ratios in the NTSC system are as follows:

$$Red = 30\% \text{ luminance} : 70\% \text{ chrominance}$$
$$Green = 59\% \text{ luminance} : 41\% \text{ chrominance}$$
$$Blue = 11\% \text{ luminance} : 89\% \text{ chrominance}$$

As each camera chip or pickup tube receives light, the voltage output is divided according to these chrominance and luminance percentages. For example, if the output from red is 1 full volt of video, then $\frac{3}{10}$ of a volt would be the amount of luminance and $\frac{7}{10}$ of a volt would be the amount of chrominance that the chip is seeing. The combination of the three television primaries in the above proportions will give white.

To separate the luminance information from the chrominance, the other side of the mathematical calculation above is used. Red is defined as 30% luminance and 70% chrominance. Therefore, 30% of whatever voltage is detected at the output of the red chip represents the luminance information. White is the sum of 30% of the output of the red chip, 59% of the green, and 11% of the blue. This signal is transmitted as the black and white information on the main picture carrier frequency. The symbol to represent luminance in video is the letter Y. Black and white receivers use only this information and do not decode the color information that is interwoven in the main carrier.

Color Difference Signals

The calculations used to create the luminance signal are also used to create the chroma or chrominance information. The color information minus the luminance information is known as the *color difference signal*. Mathematically, this would be shown as Red-Y (Red minus luminance), Green-Y, and Blue-Y, or R-Y, G-Y, and

B-Y. Based on the Pythagorean theorem, only two signals are needed to calculate the color information. R-Y and B-Y were chosen because they contain the least amount of luminance information and therefore conserve bandwidth.

The color difference signals for transmission are created by measuring the output of the red and blue chips and the luminance signal. This results in vectors which appear 90° apart from each other, creating two sides of a right triangle—on a vectorscope, the R-Y axis goes straight north and the B-Y axis goes straight east (Figure 6.5).

Once the color information from the red and blue outputs has been measured, simple arithmetic dictates what the green output is

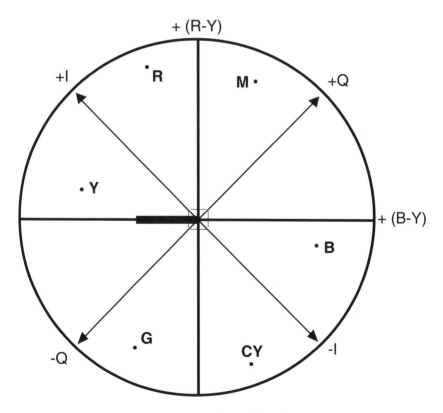

Figure 6.5 Vector Display

without actually having the information on the received signal. This process is known as *encoding* and *decoding* color.

At any given instant, knowing the vector length and angle, circuits in the receiver can reconstruct the original strengths of the R-Y and B-Y signals that produced it. From these two signals and Y, the G-Y signal can be calculated. The color television picture is then produced by combining each of the color difference signals, according to the defined percentages, with the luminance information that was on the video carrier.

I and Q Vectors

There is, however, a better way of encoding the colors than using the R-Y and B-Y axes method. In the NTSC system, it was discovered that truer representation of colors would occur if the encoding process was changed slightly. Instead of the encoding taking place along the 0° to 180° line and the 90° to 270° line with respect to burst, the colors are encoded along two different lines. One line runs from 57° to 237° from burst and is more closely aligned with the colors to which the eye is most sensitive. The vector that lies along this line is known as the *inphase vector* or *I vector*. The other line, which must be 90° away from the I vector, runs from 147° to 327° from burst. This is called the *quadrature vector* or *Q vector* (Figure 6.5).

Both the I and Q vectors have a positive and a negative portion. The portions that appear between burst and 180° are positive. Those that appear from 180° back to burst are negative. The minus I axis is 237° from the reference burst. The positive Q axis is 147° from the reference burst. In a color bar test signal, the I and Q vector signals are represented as two dark blue chips at the bottom of the screen (Figure 6.6).

Broadcast signals are encoded along the I and Q axes as opposed to the R-Y/B-Y axes. This gives truer and more accurate reproduction of color. However, the circuitry needed to encode and decode I and Q signals is more complex than the simple 90° relationship where

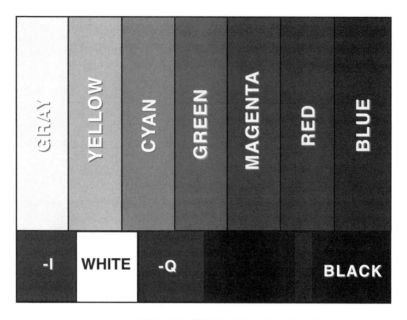

Figure 6.6 EIA Split Field Color Bar Display

B-Y is on the same axis as burst and R-Y is 90° from that. So most inexpensive monitors, and all home receivers, decode using the R-Y/B-Y method.

Other Color Standards

PAL and SECAM share the same line frequency and frame rate, which is different than NTSC. PAL and SECAM are different from each other, and from NTSC, in the way each processes color. In the PAL system, the color difference signals are encoded on two separate subcarriers. This differs from NTSC, which encodes both color difference signals on one subcarrier. By using two subcarriers 90° apart in time from each other, color phase errors, which appear in NTSC as a change in hue, appear in PAL as a slight desaturation of the color image. There is no adjustment in the PAL color system for saturation. That aspect of the signal is fixed. Because of this encoding process, color in the PAL system is truer and more consistent than it is in NTSC.

In SECAM, color difference signals are encoded one at a time in sequence on one color subcarrier signal. The receiver stores the first color difference signal, awaits the second, combines both, and creates the color image. Because each of the color difference signals is handled separately, a greater quantity of information can be encoded. As both color signals are stored within the receiver and then decoded, the color achieved is the best of all three standards.

CHAPTER 7

Monitoring the Color Image

Unlike television receivers at home, which are set to personal preferences of brightness, contrast, and color, professional monitors must be set to specifications that have been determined by the NTSC, PAL, or SECAM standard. Using a professional standard to set up a video monitor is the only way to ensure that the image that is viewed on a monitor is an exact visual representation of the electronic video signal.

The color monitor is in the group of test equipment used to judge the quality of a video image. Adjustments made to a monitor do not affect the video signal itself, but only the monitor is used as a reference to view the video image. Other test equipment is used to view different aspects of the video signal. These will be covered in the chapters that follow.

The Human Eye

The human eye is not an absolute measuring device; it is an averaging device. Eyes, like noses, get desensitized when exposed for too long to the same stimulus. As a result of looking at one or more colors for a long period of time, mistakes can easily be made when trying to color balance a video image. During setup, it can be helpful to look away periodically for a few seconds so the eyes don't become desensitized. In the case of a long setup procedure, it might be best to walk away for a few minutes into a different room with different light. It is imperative to always apply setup procedures to the monitor in the same light conditions that will be used when viewing the video image.

Color Bars

The test signal used to set up a video monitor is called color bars. It is the international professional reference used to ensure that the color of the images that follow look the same on any monitor as they did when they were created. The color bar signal contains everything needed to set up a color monitor, including color chips representing each primary and secondary color, analog or digital black, white, and reference chips for gray (Figure 7.1).

There are several varieties of color bar displays approved by the International Organization for Standardization, or IOS, the agency that sets international standards. Different color bars have different elements. For example, some color bar displays do not have a black reference chip; other color bar displays have multiple black reference chips. Some displays have more than one white reference chip. Although the elements may differ, all color bar signals have the same basic chrominance and luminance references.

The Monochrome Image

As discussed in the previous chapter, the three components of a video image are luminance, chrominance, and hue. In order to set the color aspects of the monitor properly, it is essential that the black and white (luminance) aspect of the monitor be set first as a base or reference. The principle is that video is an additive color system and white is created when all three primary colors are in proper balance. Therefore, the initial step in setting up a color video monitor is to ensure the purity of white. It must not have a color tint, but be pure white. Once this is set, the color video monitor will be in correct color balance.

Since the color information is encoded on a separate carrier, it is possible on some monitors to turn off the color burst, removing color information from the image and giving a pure monochrome image. Once the image is monochrome, the contrast control must be adjusted to display a bright image. However, if the contrast is

EIA Split Field Bars

Full Field Bars

Figure 7.1 Color Bar Displays

too high, the whites will "bloom" or bleed into the darker parts of the picture. Once contrast is set, the brightness should be adjusted to account for the ambient light in the room. The brightness of the monitor should be reduced when viewing in a darker environment and increased when the ambient light is bright.

On the monitor, the color bar image will appear as four grey bars separated by three black bars the I and Q chips if using EIA split field bars, and black. As the hue control is adjusted, the inner two bars will change, becoming lighter or darker. On some monitors, the hue control may be labeled "phase." The hue or phase must be adjusted until the inner two bars appear the same. Adjusting the saturation or chroma control will affect the two outer bars. Phase and saturation must be adjusted until all four bars appear the same.

To aid in setting the color balance, some monitors have a switch marked "Blue Only." This switch is designed to turn off the red and green displays, and simultaneously change the remaining image to monochrome. Therefore, the image, while using the blue-only display, will appear monochrome.

PLUGE Bars

There is another color bar display that is helpful in setting up a color monitor. These bars are referred to as PLUGE bars, stands for Picture Line Up Generating Equipment. PLUGE bars contain the standard color bar pattern, plus two additional references. The first reference is a set of three color chips and one white chip separated by three black chips going across the lower third of the screen (Figure 7.2). The second reference is two additional black chips within the larger black chip in the lower right-hand corner of the screen.

The four chips that appear across the lower third of the screen are used for setting the hue and saturation of the monitor. The four chips—blue, magenta, cyan, and white—each separated by black, are in the reverse order from the color bars. All four chips contain the color blue. With the red and green displays turned off, there is a blue chip under each of the blue bars. Without PLUGE bars, it was

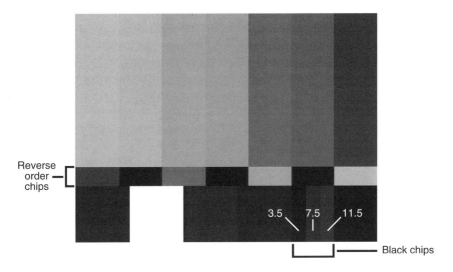

Figure 7.2 PLUGE Bar Signal

necessary to scan the entire monitor and try to balance the four color bars against each other across the screen. With the use of the PLUGE bar signal, the eye does not have to cover such a wide area when comparing signals.

Use the hue and saturation controls as above to make all the blue bars, and the chips underneath them, the same. The additional black chips in the black field aid in setting brightness. One chip is 3.5 units of video, or blacker than analog black. The other is 11.5 units, or dark grey. These are in addition to the 7.5 units of analog black.

The proper brightness for the monitor can be set by adjusting the brightness control until the 11.5-unit chip is just barely visible. If the brightness is set too high, the 3.5-unit chip becomes visible. If the brightness is set lower than the point at which the 11.5-unit chip is just visible, the colors will appear dull and the picture dark.

Color Image

If everything was adjusted correctly, the white chip in the color bar image will appear pure white without a hue and the black will appear pure black with no color shading. Once a good mono-chrome image has been set, the next step is to restore color to the monitor. Whatever procedure was used to turn color off should now be reversed to turn color back on. Color bars continue to be used as the video input signal and color reference.

Some monitors have a switch marked Set Up. This switch collapses the vertical drive so that the picture is reduced to a line or bar across the tube. This acts as an aid in setting up the basic balance of the three colors. However, the reduced scan may have a different color balance than the full picture, and therefore may not be totally reliable.

Once the monitor is set up correctly, the details of the electronic video signal can be viewed on scopes.

CHAPTER 8

Analog Waveform Monitors

A video monitor is used to judge the quality of an image. Electronic measuring tools known as *oscilloscopes* are used to measure the video signal itself. There are two types of oscilloscopes used to measure the signal, the *waveform monitor* and the *vectorscope* (Figure 8.1). This chapter covers the analog waveform monitor.

The waveform monitor is used to make sure the video signal is being recorded or reproduced within legal broadcast specifications. The following information about waveform measurements applies to all models of waveform monitors, even though the layout of buttons and switches may be different. There also may be some switches on certain waveform monitors that are not described here.

When analyzing the video signal on a waveform monitor, the view of the signal can be changed and certain parts enlarged in order to take measurements. The video signal is not affected as you take these measurements. If the video signal needs to be adjusted to meet broadcast requirements, those changes are made on the video source itself (i.e., the camera, VTR, and so on).

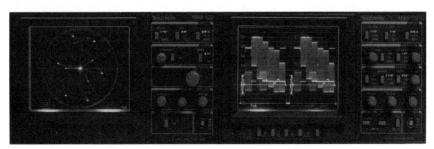

Figure 8.1 Waveform and Vectorscope Monitors

Graticule

All waveform monitors have a small *CRT* (Cathode Ray Tube) that displays an electronic representation of the video image. In front of the CRT is a glass or plastic plate known as the CRT *graticule*. The CRT graticule is made up of vertical and horizontal lines used to measure the video signal. The horizontal lines are in *IRE units* of video. These measurements were first developed by the Institute of Radio Engineers (IRE) and are therefore referred to as IRE units of measurement. The IRE scale ranges from −40 to 100 units. The measurement from −40 to 100 IRE is referred to as one volt of video peak-to-peak (Figure 8.2).

The horizontal line at zero units is referred to as the *base line* (Figure 8.2). It is marked with vertical divisions in microseconds and tenths

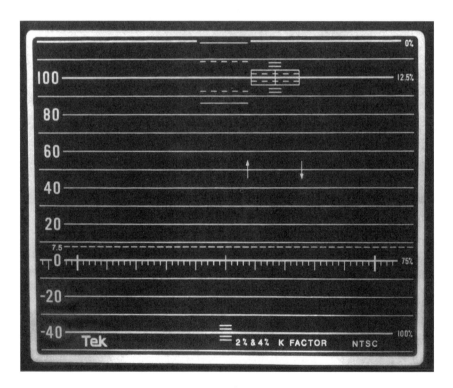

Figure 8.2 Waveform Graticule

of microseconds. The shortest vertical lines represent $\frac{2}{10}$ of a microsecond, and at every fifth $\frac{2}{10}$ of a microsecond is a slightly taller line that represents a 1-microsecond division, or 1. There are two taller lines near opposite ends of the base line which represent a 10 microsecond division. These are used in measuring horizontal blanking.

Signal Components on Graticule

When reading a composite signal on the waveform, the zero-units line of the video signal is always set on the base line of the graticule. The *horizontal sync pulse* should be at the −40-units line beneath the base line. The color burst portion of the signal should reach from −20 IRE units to +20 IRE units, for a total of 40 IRE units (Figure 8.3).

The active video signal, when viewed as luminance only, occupies the range between 7.5 units and 100 units on the monitor. In Figure 8.3, the white portion of the video color bars generates the top part of the waveform display. The horizontal line near the top of the graticule, which should match the pure white color bar signal, is equal to 100 units. Black, which is also referred to as setup or pedestal, is the darkest part of the signal and should be on the 7.5-units dotted line, 2.5 units below the 10-unit line. A proper 100% video signal will measure 140 units on the graticule scale from the horizontal sync to the white peaks. Again, horizontal sync takes up the portion between −40 and 0 units, while the active video image extends from 7.5 to 100 units on the scale.

Waveform Display Controls

There are different models of waveform monitors. Some have dedicated controls while others have programmable controls. To clearly introduce the concepts of a waveform monitor, the Tektronix 1730 waveform monitor, with dedicated controls, will be used as a reference. On the Tektronix 1730, there are five sections with controls that are used to operate the waveform monitor (Figure 8.3). Two waveform display controls affect the placement of the signal

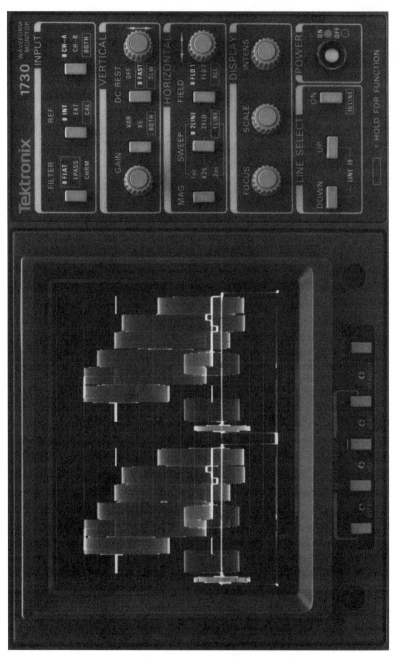

Figure 8.3 Waveform Monitor

against the IRE scale on the graticule. These two controls are used to position the video signal against the graticule so that accurate measurements can be taken.

For example, if the placement of the waveform monitor is above eye level, the video signal will appear differently against the graticule than if it is below eye level. The Vertical control (within section 2 in Figure 8.3) moves the display of the video display up or down against the graticule, or measurement scale. The Horizontal control (within section 3 in Figure 8.3) moves the waveform display to the left or right against the graticule.

In section 4 of Figure 8.3, there are three additional display controls. The FOCUS control is used to focus whatever signal is on the CRT display. The SCALE control makes the graticule brighter or darker. The INTENSITY control makes the CRT display brighter or darker. Beneath the Intensity control is the power switch, which turns the waveform monitor on and off.

Signal Measurement

In section 3 in Figure 8.3, the second button from the left is the SWEEP selection. The word *sweep* refers to the display of the video signal on the CRT. If the SWEEP button is pressed, either a two-line horizontal display or a two-field vertical display will be shown. If the SWEEP button is held in, the signal will convert to a line display. The line display, when used in conjunction with section 5 LINE SELECT, will allow viewing of single scan lines.

The button on the far left of section 3 is marked MAG and is used to magnify the display for more precise measurements. It can be used in conjunction with the SWEEP button. Once the type of display has been selected with the SWEEP button, the MAG allows the selection of magnification. The one-microsecond selection (1µs) is the usual display for most viewing and measuring purposes. The second selection will expand the sweep by 25 times (X25) for very precise measurements. The third selection is .2-microsecond divisions (.2µs) which is usually used for measuring blanking. Any of the magnification selections may be used in either the two-line or two-field displays.

If the one LINE choice is selected, then the controls in section 5 will be useful. The ON button must be used to activate the line selector. The use of the UP and DOWN buttons allows the viewing of any individual line in a field.

Depressing the UP and DOWN buttons together will automatically display line 19. Line 19 is the last line of inactive video in the vertical blanking interval and may contain test signals or data. Holding the ON button will automatically display any successive 15 lines, which can be overlaid from the A and B channels for matching video sources.

The third button in section 3 selects either Field 1 (FLD 1) or Field 2 (FLD 2) or both fields (ALL) simultaneously.

When it is necessary to look more closely at part of a signal, the GAIN knob in section 2 can be used to expand the signal. When used in conjunction with the button to its right, the sweep may be expanded vertically. With the Variable position selected (VAR), the GAIN knob will control the height of the display from approximately 25% of normal to approximately 150% of normal. If X5 is selected, the sweep will be expanded to 5 times its normal height. If the button is held in, the signal will expand to 5 times normal and the GAIN knob will allow the sweep to be adjusted via the knob from that point.

Filters

In section 1 of Figure 8.3, the button marked FILTER selects the content of the display as far as luminance and chrominance are concerned. A FLAT display shows the luminance and chrominance of the signal combined. Low Pass (LPASS) selects the luminance portion of the signal only. Likewise, chrominance (CHRM) selects the color portion of the signal alone. Holding in the FILTER button will display one half of the sweep as luminance and chrominance combined (or flat) and one half of the sweep as luminance only (Figure 8.4).

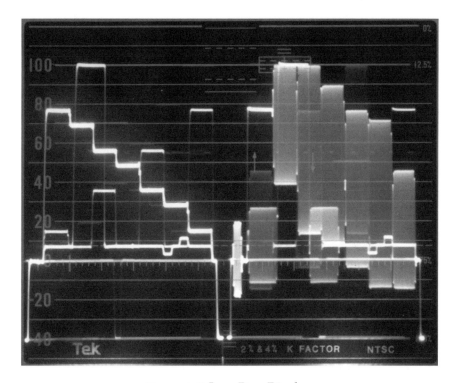

Figure 8.4 Low Pass Display

Reference

The reference button (REF) is used to select either an internal or external reference. External reference (EXT) is used to synchronize the scope with individual pieces of equipment and is helpful when timing in a room. The internal reference (INT) synchronizes the oscilloscope display with an internal reference so the display will not shift when a different source is selected.

Holding in the REF button will turn on the *calibration pulse*. The calibration pulse is used to determine if the scope is properly set for taking measurements. The entire 140-unit video signal is equal to an electrical strength of one volt peak-to-peak. As long as the calibration pulse equals 140 units, or one volt, the scope is calibrated correctly.

If the calibration pulse shows the display to be anything other than 140 units, there are controls in section 6 which can adjust it. Use of the controls marked VCAL and HCAL will allow the scope to be adjusted horizontally or vertically until it is correct. Once calibrated, the scope can then be used reliably for measuring.

Inputs

The button on the far right of section 1 selects inputs to the waveform monitor. One waveform monitor may be connected to two sources so that they share one scope. With this button you may select either source, or view both at the same time.

In section 2, the button on the far right, *D.C. Restoration* (DC REST), is used to keep the signal from drifting on the face of the CRT. In the OFF position, the sweep will drift up or down as sources that are feeding the scope are selected or changed. Selection of FAST or SLW (slow) will keep the scope locked in one position regardless of the source.

Display

Under the CRT, in addition to the VCAL and HCAL controls, there is a control for rotating the sweep in the event the display is tilted. The four RECALL SET UP buttons on the left, when used with the STORE button on the right, allow the storage of up to four different setups of the scope. A stored setup includes any arrangements, settings, or selections made on the scope. These setups can be recalled at any time. The control marked READ OUT operates the alpha numeric readout on the CRT.

Combining Setups

Most of the selections of buttons can and will be used in combination with each other. For example, to measure the horizontal blanking period, a combination might be to select FLAT on the filter, INT (internal reference), CH-A, D.C. REST FAST, sweep set for 2 LINE and .2μs (.2-microsecond divisions). This display will allow the measurement of the horizontal sync pulse, the burst, and the internal measurements of each portion of the entire horizontal blanking period. The vertical blanking period can be measured by changing the sweep to 2FLD (2 Field) and leaving the other settings the same. Blanking measurement is discussed in more detail in Chapter 20, Operations Overview.

To check the strength of the signal, change the .2μs to 1μs and the filter to LPASS. This will allow accurate measurement of the luminance portion of the signal to see that is does not exceed 100 units nor go below 7½ units.

While different scopes can have different configurations of controls, the same settings may be accomplished and the same measurements taken with any waveform monitor.

Viewing Color Bars

The color bar signal represents the output of a playback device. It displays each of the primary and secondary colors that make up the video signal. It also provides a reference for black and white levels. Adjusting video levels on scopes using color bars as a reference ensures proper reproduction of the signal that follows.

As a test signal, colors bars are designed as a reference for the setup of playback devices and monitors. True video generally does not reach the levels that are contained in a color bar pattern, because color bars by their intent are designed to indicate the limits of the signal (i.e., the highest luminance level, the highest chrominance level, the lowest luminance, and so on). If the colors were presented in the color bar display at 100% of their true values, the reference signals would be beyond the measuring capabilities of the analog waveform monitor. For example, SMPTE defines yellow as 133 IRE units when fully saturated. The graticule on the analog waveform does not measure beyond 120 IRE units. For this reason, a color bar signal reduced to 75% of true levels was created, and this 75% color bars the general standard in use. The yellow bar in the 75% color bar display appears as 100 IRE units.

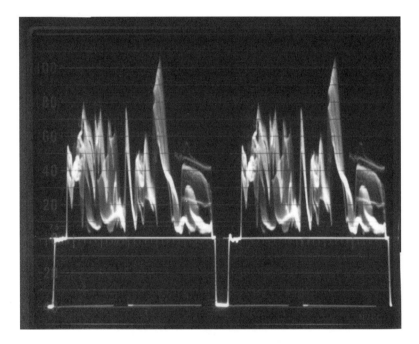

Figure 8.5 Image on Waveform

Viewing an Image

A color bar signal contains precise amounts and durations of chrominance and luminance that appear in an ordered fashion. This signal is used to ensure the video images that follow will fall within the specifications of a specific standard. However, when video images are viewed on a waveform monitor, the scope reflects the chrominance and luminance levels of the video image, which never appear as precise and ordered as color bar signals. Often, there is a wide variety of image elements spread over the peaks and valleys of the entire signal range (Figure 8.5).

Some digital cameras, imaging software, and nonlinear editing applications have representations called *histograms*. Histograms are waveform displays of the pixels in an image and appear similar to how the image looks on a video waveform monitor. The brighter pixels or picture elements appear toward the upper range of the histogram and the darker pixels appear toward the lower range.

CHAPTER 9
Analog Vectorscopes

The *vectorscope* is another type of oscilloscope used in measuring the video signal. Unlike the waveform monitor, which measures the luminance aspects of a video signal, a vectorscope is used to measure the hue.

The vectorscope, like the waveform monitor, is made up of a CRT, graticule, and knobs and buttons. The lines and markings on the graticule are used as the framework under which the chrominance of the signal is displayed for reference. The controls adjust the placement of the chrominance display pattern. Other vectorscopes may have controls in a different configuration, but the functions detailed in this chapter will be available on all models. To clearly introduce the concepts of a vectorscope, the Tektronix 1720, with dedicated controls, will be used as a reference.

Graticule

As with waveform monitors, vectorscopes have a small CRT that displays the signal. The CRT lies behind a glass or plastic plate inscribed with a circle that has markings and lines, which is the graticule (Figure 9.1). The markings on the circle itself represent degrees from 0 to 360. The thinner, individual notches or markings represent differences of 2°. The bolder markings represent 10° intervals. The 0° point or mark is at a nine o'clock position on the scope. The degree markings move in a clockwise position from that point.

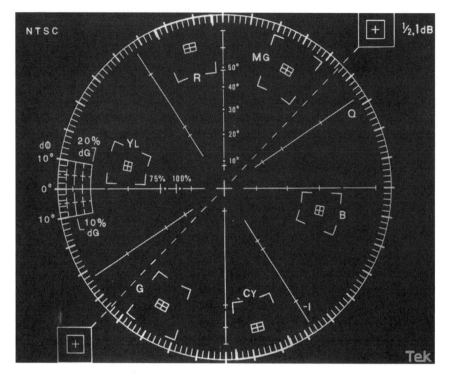

Figure 9.1 Vectorscope Graticule

Axes

There are two perpendicular lines that cut horizontally and vertically through the circle. The line that goes from 0° to 180° is referred to as the *X axis*. The up and down line that goes from 90° to 270° is called the *Y axis*. The *Q axis* is in the upper right-hand quadrant, and the *-I axis* is in the lower right quadrant of the circle.

Vector Readings

On the graticule, there are individual boxes that are located within the circle. Starting from the nine o'clock position and moving clockwise, these are yellow (YL), red (R), magenta (MG), blue (B), cyan (CY), and green (G). The three primary colors, red, blue, and green, are each separated by one of the secondary colors. The secondary color is a mixture of the two primary colors on either side of it. The box placement represents the direction or hue of a particular vector. The boxes are also used as an indication of the correct length of a vector, or its saturation.

The small boxes that are indicated for each color are correct SMPTE/NTSC specifications for the phase and amplitude of that particular color in the color bar test signal. The larger box that surrounds each small box is the allowable range that a color can vary in transmission and still be considered correct. If a color does not meet the exact specification, but is within tolerance, it is considered acceptable for test purposes.

The proper setup of the chrominance signal for color bars should show the center point of the signal aligned with the center point of the circle scale. The burst of the color subcarrier signal, the short line on the X axis, should point directly to the nine o'clock position. Much like a video image on the waveform, the color bars are designed to fit into specific color boxes in the vectorscope. Viewing the video image of a signal other than color bars will not appear as exact or ordered as the color bar test signal appears.

Setup Controls

Using as a reference the Tektronix 1730, the controls for general setup and adjustment of the vectorscope are on the right-hand side (Figure 9.2), and are divided into six sections. Section 4 has three knobs. The knob farthest to the left is FOCUS, for making the signal as sharp and clear as possible. The knob to the right of the focus is SCALE which controls scale illumination or the brightness of the graticule. The knob to the right of that is INTENS which controls the intensity of the waveform picture on the CRT.

Directly above the INTENS knob is the PHASE control, which rotates the whole display clockwise or counter-clockwise. Directly beneath the intensity knob is the POWER switch, which turns the vectorscope on and off.

Figure 9.2 Vectorscope

Section 2 has two controls. The BARS button on the right adjusts the size of the vector display depending on the type of color bar display being viewed. The standard SMPTE color bars in their various configurations (full field, EIA split field, PLUGE, etc.) are a 75% test signal. If the test bars being used are a 100% signal, which is an option on a color bar generator, they will not fit the vectorscope unless this button is used.

To the left of the BARS button is the VARIABLE control. If the VARIABLE button is pressed, the knob can be used to vary the size of the display. This is useful when trying to time in or synchronize a piece of equipment. By enlarging the display, any variation in phase between two sources will be easier to see. The VARIABLE button is usually left OFF unless this adjustment needs to be made.

Input Selections

Section 1 has three buttons. The one on the left marked MODE will select a standard vector display. If MODE is pressed, it will switch the display to an X/Y or R-Y/B-Y mode. In this mode, all the vectors are compressed into those two vectors. Holding in the MODE button will show both displays simultaneously.

The center button marked REF, for reference, is used to select the synchronizing source for the vectorscope. When INT or internal is selected, the scope will supply its own synchronizing signal. If switched to EXT or external, it will use the external source feeding it for its synchronization. When timing in pieces of equipment, the switch should be set on EXT so that any differences between the various pieces of equipment will be seen.

If the REF button is held in, two test circles will be displayed. One test circle will appear at the outer edge of the graticule circle and the other is formed by the rotation of the burst. This display, when used in conjunction with the GAIN CAL or calibration gain control under the CRT, is used to calibrate or adjust the vectorscope. It is the equivalent of the calibration pulse on the waveform monitor.

The button on the far right of section 1 selects one of two inputs that are available to the scope. The two inputs are referred to as CH-A and CH-B or Channel A and Channel B. Having two inputs is helpful in situations where one scope is shared by two machines. Holding in the BOTH button will display both inputs simultaneously.

In section 3, to the left of the PHASE control knob, is a button marked SC/H, which stands for *Subcarrier/Horizontal phasing*. The principles of subcarrier/horizontal phasing are discussed in Chapter 20, Operations Overview. Pressing the SC/H button will show a small dot on the vectorscope at the left edge of the circle opposite the burst. The position of this dot will indicate if the signal feeding the scope is properly SC/H phased, and if it is not, how far out of phase it is.

In section 5, a button marked AUXILIARY can display the matching vector readout of the selections made on the Tektronix 1730 waveform monitor if both scopes are connected and used together.

Calibration

Under the CRT in section 6 are four adjustments for the display itself. The control on the far left, ROTATE, will rotate the display very much like the phase knob. However, this adjustment is meant for setting up the scope, rather than rotating, for purposes of comparison between signals.

The next control to the right is GAIN CAL for calibrating the size of the display. It can be used in conjunction with the REF button in section 1. In this manner, the display can be adjusted so that it can be used to accurately measure vectors.

The two controls on the right of section 6 will move the display up or down and left or right. Using the point where the vectors come together as the center of the display, these controls allow the movement of the display to be in the center of the graticule.

Active Video

During active video, the vectors will not be quite so straight because they represent the variety of colors in the television picture rather than the pure colors that exist in a color bar signal.

PAL Signal

The PAL color difference signals are encoded on two separate subcarriers. On a vectorscope, the signal appears with two sets of color information, appearing like a double NTSC signal (Figure 9.3).

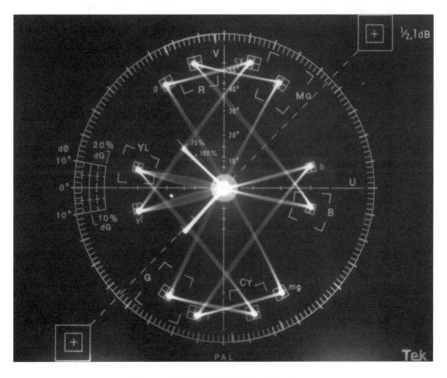

Figure 9.3 PAL Vector Display

Other Scopes

To minimize cost and equipment space, current scopes combine waveform and vectorscopes and even audio signals into one scope. Rather than having dedicated buttons and knobs, these scopes have soft keys that are menu driven (Figure 9.4).

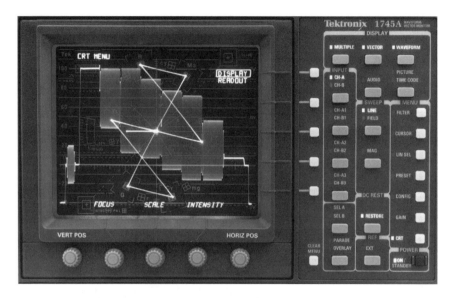

Figure 9.4 Dual Scope

Scopes will continue to vary in design from manufacturer to manufacturer and will continue to add additional features. However, all will use the current standards and measuring guides.

CHAPTER 10
The Encoded Signal

Video information is constrained by available transmission bandwidth and the limitations of recording media. To overcome this limitation, the video information must first be condensed or compressed so it will fit within the available space. This is done through a process called *encoding*, which involves taking all the parts of the video and audio information and combining or eliminating the redundant material mathematically. It is also the process of converting from one form of information, such as light, to another form, such as electrical or magnetic data, for use in recording and transmitting video and audio signals.

Analog and Digital Encoding

There are four ways to encode or process video signals. In both the analog and digital domains, there are component outputs and composite outputs available. While they are both referred to the same way in each domain, the processing is different for analog than it is for digital, thus yielding four distinct ways to process video signals. They are analog composite, analog component, digital composite, and digital component. Originally, all television broadcasting was composite analog. With the advent of digital processing, more and more broadcasting is becoming digital. As digital broadcasting becomes the standard, the majority of signal processing will be digital component.

Analog Encoding Process

As mentioned above, there are different ways to encode a signal. The NTSC color process is one form of encoding. As an example, when color was added to the black and white signal, that information was encoded so it would fit within the existing transmission and recording systems. This was done using the Pythagorean theorem (Figure 10.1).

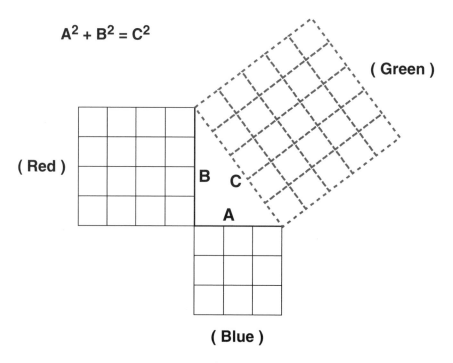

Figure 10.1 Pythagorean Theorem

The Pythagorean theorem is an equation in plane geometry that states that if the two sides of a right triangle (a triangle that contains a 90° angle) are known, the length of the third side can be calculated. The mathematical formula for this is $A^2 + B^2 = C^2$. In the NTSC video signal, green is 59% of the luminance signal, red is 30% luminance, and blue is 11% luminance. When the red and blue signals are combined, they contain less luminance information

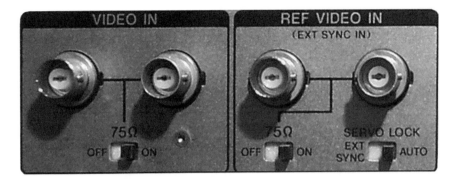

Figure 10.2 Analog Composite Input/Output

than green alone. Therefore, if the red and blue signals are timed to appear 90° apart from each other, the third side of the triangle (green) can be mathematically derived, thereby eliminating the green signal (Figure 10.1). The video color information in this encoded signal is thereby reduced or condensed by more than half.

Luminance is encoded by modulating a carrier frequency in both the recording and transmitting process. The light or luminance information is converted to electrical signals that are then used to change or modulate a carrier signal. Light information is also converted to magnetic and optical data for recording purposes, which are additional forms of encoded signals.

Analog Composite Signal

In the analog domain, there are two types of signal processing: composite and component. The composite signal is the combination of all the elements that make up the video signal. This information includes luminance (Y), the color difference signals (R-Y, B-Y), and synchronizing information (H, V, and color). This information is recorded and played back as one signal (Figure 10.2). Because of the limitations of recording space and the quantity of information contained in a composite signal, this information is encoded to reduce the quantity of data.

In recording, the composite video is encoded while the audio is a direct recorded signal (non-encoded). In transmission, both audio and video signals are encoded. They are, however, transmitted separately. The video encoded signal is transmitted through the AM (Amplitude Modulation) process and the audio encoded signal is transmitted through the FM (Frequency Modulation) process.

By reversing the mathematical process used to encode, the signal is *decoded*, or recreated, in its original form for viewing on a video monitor. The encoding and decoding process by its very nature induces certain errors and unwanted signals. Every time a recording, dub, or edited master is created, the composite signal goes through encoding and decoding, sometimes several times, resulting in a number of undesirable elements that degrade the picture quality.

Analog Component Signal

All of the signals that are transmitted in the analog domain are composite in that all of the elements necessary (luminance, chrominance, and synchronization) are combined in one signal. However, in the analog component system, the luminance and chrominance signals may be recorded separately. The chrominance information is recorded as the individual color difference signals, R-Y and B-Y. Each of these signals appears as a separate input and output to the recording device. The luminance signal (Y) is recorded separately and also appears as an individual input and output (Figure 10.3).

The advantage of keeping the elements separate is that a higher quality of image can be maintained. By recording in this manner, less encoding and decoding is required, thus reducing the loss of fidelity and retaining the original quality. By keeping the signals in a component or non-encoded form, it is possible to go through many generations without much loss of signal quality.

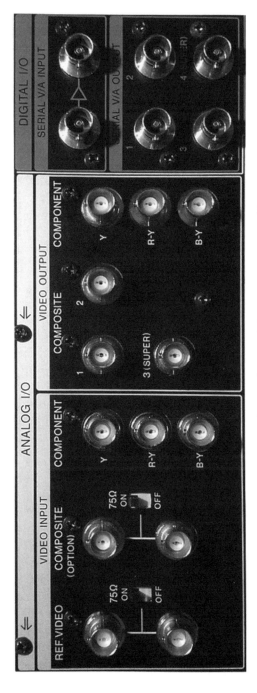

Figure 10.3 Analog and Digital Component Input/Output

Digital Encoding Process

Encoding is used in the digital domain to accomplish the same purposes as in analog, i.e., reduce the bandwidth for transmission and recording. Digital encoding is the process of converting analog information to digital data. In this manner, a very large amount of analog information can be reduced to a simple stream of digital data.

In the digital domain, there is an added advantage in that encoded information can be processed at a higher rate of speed. With an increase in speed, more information can be processed, thereby allowing all three color signals to be handled without the need for mathematically condensing and extracting the information.

To differentiate between analog and digital, the reference to the color difference signals in the digital domain was changed from the analog notation of R-Y, B-Y to P_B, P_R or $C_B C_R$. The notation of $P_B P_R$ is used to indicate the encoding and transferring of analog signals into the digital domain. The notation used for encoding and transferring the color difference signals within the digital domain is written as $C_B C_R$. The reference to luminance remains Y. When the complete signal is notated, it appears as $YP_B P_R$ or $YC_B C_R$.

Digital Composite Signals

Digital composite video is very similar to composite analog with the only difference being that the information is recorded, stored, and transmitted as digital data rather than analog waveforms. A digital composite signal takes the complete video signal, with all of its elements combined, and records or transmits it in a digital form. As in the analog composite signal, the combined elements of a digital composite signal include, luminance (Y), color difference signals (P_B, P_R), and synchronizing information (H, V, and color) Figure 10.4.

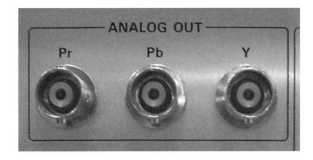

Figure 10.4 Analog Out

Digital Component Signal

Digital component video takes the elements that comprise a digital video signal (YC_BC_R) and keeps them separate in recording and transmission. This is similar to analog component in the way these elements are treated.

However, in digital component video, there is an additional option. It is possible to record the pure outputs of the red (R), green (G), and blue (B) channels, and the luminance (Y) information rather than the color difference signals (C_BC_R). The integrity of each element is retained and the resulting quality is the cleanest and closest to the original signals of all the possible encoding options. The RGBY signals are direct outputs of each of the channels, as opposed to the YC_BC_R which are derived from the mathematically encoded components.

The inputs and outputs from digital cameras and recording devices can either be RGBY or the YC_BC_R components. Equipment that is capable of creating or reproducing these digital elements will have separate wires for each of these elements. In the case of the RGBY, there will be four separate wires. In the case of YC_BC_R, there will be three separate wires.

Transcoding

Because there are several standards and recording devices, it is necessary at times to translate from one type of encoded video signal to another type of encoded video signal. This process is known as *transcoding*. For example, a digital composite or component signal can be transcoded to an analog composite or component signal, or vice versa. An RGBY video signal, which is generated by a video camera, can be transcoded into an analog or digital component YP_B, P_R or YC_BC_R video signal for input or output.

Encoding and Compression

Signal encoding is an aspect of the recording and transmission process. While it allows for some compression of the signals, its main purpose is to facilitate the recording and transmission of these signals. The encoding process contains elements of signal compression, but is not the same as the compression process in the digital domain. Compression is covered in Chapter 15.

CHAPTER 11

Digital Theory

An analog signal is a sine wave. Like an ocean wave in constant motion, an analog signal continually changes over time. In fact, the term analog is actually derived from the word analogous because of the signal's analogous relationship to the sine wave (Figure 11.1). Digital information, on the other hand, is fixed and absolute and does not change over time. When information is digitized, the data remains as it was originally recorded.

Analog Video

Video was originally developed as part of the analog world. Because the system was analog, it had the ease and advantages of fitting into the natural physical system. However, it also carried with it all the interference and noise problems. Noise is analog information just as video and audio are. Getting rid of noise and interference in the analog video signal is not easy, as they take the

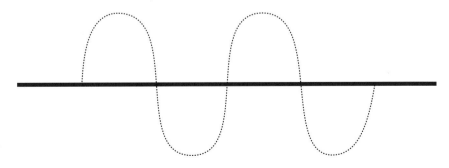

Figure 11.1 Sine Wave

same form as the video and audio signals. Also, manipulating analog information for creative purposes is complex.

To eliminate interference problems and make better creative use of video, a process of digitizing video signals was created. Digitizing refers to converting the analog information to a series of numbers. As digital information, the signals are not subject to real-world analog interference. Real-world physical problems have no effect on the television signal when it is digitized. Also, digitizing allows for a much more creative use of the video signal.

Digital Video

To create digital video, a digital representation of the analog sine wave had to be created, that is, the analog sine wave had to be *recreated* digitally. To do this, a process was developed to measure the sine wave at different times and assign a numerical value to each measurement. A sine wave curve is constantly changing over time. Therefore, the more frequently this measurement is taken, the more accurate the digital reproduction of the sine wave will be. A doctor measuring a patient's temperature once a day might not get a very accurate picture of the patient. However, taking a reading every hour will give the doctor a much clearer idea of the patient's progress.

Sampling Rate

Another way to think of digitizing is to imagine a connect-the-dots puzzle. The more dots there are to connect, the more closely the curves and outlines will reproduce the picture. The frequency of the dots, or the doctor's temperature readings, are referred to as the *sampling rate*. If the sine wave was measured every 90°, there would be three straight lines instead of a curve. However, if the sampling rate was increased to every 10°, 5°, or even every 1°, the curve of the sine wave would be more accurately represented (Figure 11.2.)

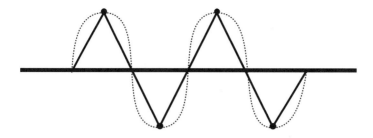

PATTERN DETERMINED FROM FOUR SAMPLES TAKEN

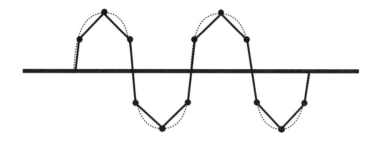

PATTERN DETERMINED FROM TWELVE SAMPLES TAKEN

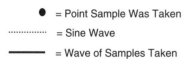
= Point Sample Was Taken

.... = Sine Wave

──────── = Wave of Samples Taken

Figure 11.2

There were two factors affecting how the sampling rate for digital video was determined. First, the sampling had to occur frequently enough to accurately reproduce the analog signal. Second, the process had to be simple enough to integrate with the existing analog system. The one element that satisfied both factors was the use of the subcarrier frequency. The subcarrier frequency was used as the basis of the sampling rate because it was the main synchronizing signal for the analog video system.

However, using a sampling rate that equals the subcarrier frequency itself does not create an accurate representation of the analog information. Therefore, it was decided that a multiple of the subcarrier could be used. The sampling rate decided on was four times the subcarrier frequency for the luminance signal and two times the subcarrier frequency for the color components.

Simple mathematics of multiplying 3.58 megahertz (color subcarrier frequency) times 4 will give a sampling rate of 14.3 megahertz. In other words, readings of the signal are taken over 14 million times a second. A value is assigned to each reading, and that number is recorded. What is recorded is not a real-world analog signal, but a series of numbers representing video and audio levels at each instant the signal was sampled.

Certain numbers keep coming up when dealing with digital equipment. For example, RS232, RS422, 4:2:2, 4:4:4, and 4:4:4:4. The RS numbers are standards for machine and computer interfaces and actually have nothing to do with the digital sampling rate. The other numbers represent digital sampling standards for video signals. For example, 4:2:2 represents four times the subcarrier frequency as the sampling rate for the luminance portion of the signal, and two times the subcarrier frequency for each of the color difference signals. 4:4:4 represents four times the subcarrier frequency for all three of those signals and 4:4:4:4 adds the key signal, or alpha channel, as part of the digital information.

Computer Processing

Early computers functioned using a series of switches that were either on or off, providing either a yes or no option. This could be likened to a questionnaire created to find out someone's name where only yes or no answers can be given, each answer represented by a 0 or 1, respectively. To give a person's name, a letter from the alphabet would be offered and the person would say yes or no to indicate whether that letter is the next letter in his or her name. They would go through the alphabet with the person answering yes or no to each letter, then repeating the process until the full name was spelled correctly. The process would be slow but accurate.

That is essentially what a computer is doing as it goes through its memory. The faster it goes through the yes and no questions, the faster it can process the information. The rate at which this information is processed is measured in megahertz and is one of the specifications that differs from computer to computer. The higher the rate as measured in megahertz (MHz), the faster the computer processor.

Binary System

Each of the yes or no answers referred to above is represented by a zero or one, or combination of zeros and ones. This is called a *binary system* because it is made up of two numbers. The binary system is used for all digitizing processes because it is the language of computers. Each zero and one is a digital or *binary bit*. The number of binary or digital bits the computer can read at once is known as the *word size*. The original computer processors were 8-bit, but soon grew to 16-bit, 32-bit, and so on. Computers continue to increase their capability of handling larger word sizes. The bigger the word size the computer can handle, the faster it can process information. The processing speed of computers continues to increase in megahertz as well. These two factors combined have been responsible for the increase in computer efficiency and speed.

Unlike the binary system, which is based on two numbers, the common mathematical system in use today is the decimal system, which uses values 0 through 9. In this system, the column on the far right represents ones, or individual units, and the next column to the left represents tens of units. The third column to the left represents hundreds of units, and the forth column, thousands of units, and so on. Each column has a value from 0 to 9. After 9, a new column is started to the left. For example, 198 is represented as an 8 in the ones column, a 9 in the tens column, and a 1 in the hundreds column. After 198 comes 199 and then 200. A 200 means there are 2 hundreds of units, 0 tens of units, and 0 individual units.

Value:	128	64	32	16	8	4	2	1		
	0	0	0	0	0	0	0	0	=	0
	0	0	0	0	0	0	0	1	=	1
	0	0	0	0	0	0	1	0	=	2
	0	0	0	0	0	0	1	1	=	3
	0	0	0	0	0	1	0	0	=	4
	0	0	0	0	0	1	0	1	=	5
	0	0	0	0	0	1	1	0	=	6
	0	0	0	0	0	1	1	1	=	7
	0	0	0	0	1	0	0	0	=	8

In the binary system, a computer does the same type of math but its columns only have values of 0 and 1. The first column represents ones or individual units. The second column to the left represents twos of units. The third column represents fours of units. The fourth column to the left represents eights of units, and so on.

Using the table above, if there is a 1 in the second column and a 0 in the first column, this indicates there is one unit of twos. The number 3 is represented by a 1 in the first column and a 1 in the second column, indicating 1 unit of twos plus 1 individual unit. The number 4 is a 1 in the third column and a 0 in both the first and second columns, indicating 1 unit of fours and 0 units of twos and ones. Five is represented by 1 unit of fours, 0 units of twos, and 1 individual unit, or 101. A 1 in each of the eight columns, or 11111111, represents the number 255. The number 256 is the start of the ninth column. Thus, the largest word that an 8-bit computer can process at a time is eight bits or one *byte*.

The language of computers is based on a code system known as ASCII (American Standard for Computer Information Interchange). In this system, there are 255 numbers, letters, and symbols, each with its own binary code. When entering data into a computer, the information is converted from analog to digital based on the ASCII codes. When you sample a video signal, the numerical equivalent that results from the measurement is converted to digital information based on the ASCII code system. This allows for universal exchange of information.

Digital Stream

Once data has been digitized, the digital bits that comprise the data can be transmitted. The form of transmission used for digital data is referred to as *serial digital*. The term serial refers to the series of binary bits that are sent out as one continuous stream of digital data, or the *digital stream*. When working with a video signal, this digital stream contains all the information about the image and audio.

The quantity of data in a digital stream dictates the quality or detail of the image. The more detail, or sampled information, from the image, the larger the quantity of data (Figure 11.3). The larger the quantity of data, the greater the amount of bandwidth required to transmit the data. This movement of data is referred to as *throughput*. The larger the bandwidth, or the greater the through-put, the greater the quantity of data that can be carried in the serial digital stream. If the bandwidth used for transmission is too small for the quantity of data being carried in the digital stream, digital bits are dropped or lost. The result is a loss of image quality. In some cases, this can result in a complete loss of the signal.

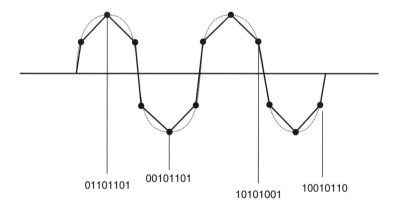

Figure 11.3 Binary Numbers Representing Samples Taken

In order for the digital stream to be received and interpreted correctly, all of the digital bits must be organized. Organizing digital data is similar to adding punctuation to a group of sentences. Without punctuation, it would be difficult or impossible to read the material and comprehend it. Digital data begins as bits, in the form of zeros and ones, which are grouped into elements called *frames*. Groups of frames are organized into *packets*. Groups of packets are organized into *segments*. The result of a group of segments is the digital stream (Figure 11.4).

Each of these elements in the digital stream is encoded so it can be received and combined in the proper order. If some of the information from the digital stream is lost from any one of these elements, the data, or image, can become unintelligible to the receiving source. In addition to data originating from one source, a serial digital stream may also contain information from several other sources. Just as a single computer is not the only active participant on the Internet, several sources transmitting various types of data may share a single transmission line. It is for this reason that the frame, packet, and segment information is critical. Without this data, there is no way to decode the serial digital stream to recreate the original data at the intended receiving source.

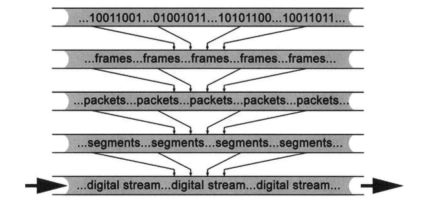

Figure 11.4 Digital Stream Data

Serial Digital Interface

The transfer of data from one source to another occurs through an *SDI*, or *serial digital interface*. This interface allows the transfer of data between sources (Figure 11.5). An SDI is sometimes a stand-alone device and sometimes it is incorporated as an integral part of a piece of equipment. An SDI input/output port can be found on cameras, VCRs, or other production or computer equipment (Figure 11.5).

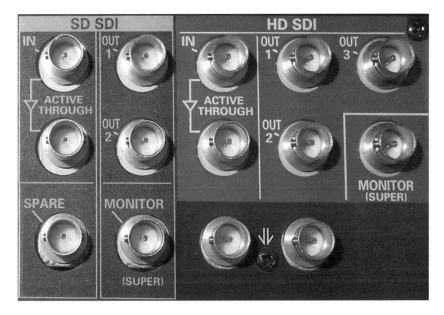

Figure 11.5 Serial Digital Interface (SDI)

In addition to the video information embedded in the digital stream is all the audio information, regardless of the number of audio channels. There are no separate wires for audio. All of the video and audio data is contained in a single serial digital stream and carried through a single SDI.

CHAPTER 12

Digital Television Standards

A standard is a set of protocols or rules that define how a system operates. Standards provide a coherent platform from which information can be created, extracted, and exchanged. Without these protocols, there would be no consistency in the handling of information. Television is the conversion of light to electrical energy. The process by which this conversion takes place is referred to as a *television standard* or system. Standards are necessary so that video signals can be created and interpreted by each piece of video equipment. For example, video levels, broadcast frequencies, subcarrier frequency, and frame rates are all dictated by a specific standard. NTSC analog is one example of a video standard. Other world standards include PAL and SECAM (Figure 12.1).

Formats are different from standards in that a format dictates the mechanical device, such as a VCR, DVD, or computer servers or hard drives, used in the creation, extraction, and exchange of information. There can be many different formats within a given standard or set of protocols.

Standards Organizations

There are several variations of digital standards. These standards are set by international agreement through various worldwide organizations, all of whom fall under the auspices of the ISO, the International Organization of Standardization. The ISO is a worldwide federation of national standards groups from some 140 countries. It is a non-government organization established in 1947 to set technical standards for scientific, technological, and economic activity.

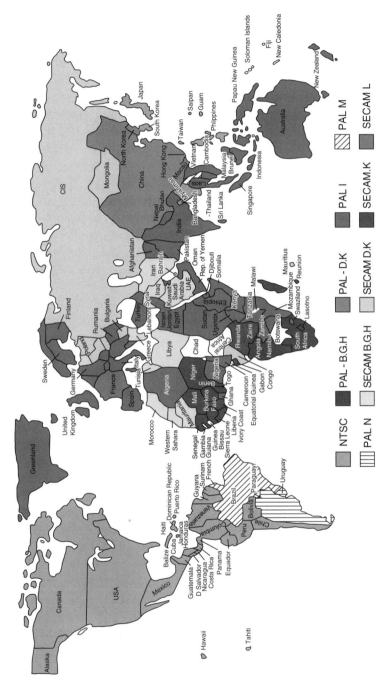

Figure 12.1 World Map of Standards

NOTE: The original world standards in analog television broadcasting included NTSC, PAL, and SECAM. There are also several subcategories of these original standards that were created and continue to be used throughout the world as you see in this illustration.

Some of the video organizations under the ISO include SMPTE, NTSC, EBU or European Broadcast Union, and the ATSC or the Advanced Television Systems Committee. These organizations have set and continue to define the technical standards for generation, distribution, and reception of video signals.

Standards Criteria

Before defining specific standards, an understanding of the basic criteria of a standard is necessary. Some of the criteria that create a standard include how many pixels make up the image (image resolution), the shape of the image (aspect ratio), the shape of the pixels that make up the image (pixel aspect ratio), the scanning process used to display the image, the audio frequency, and the number of frames displayed per second (frame rate).

Image Resolution

Image resolution is the detail or quality of the video image as it is created or displayed in a camera, video monitor, or other display source. The amount of detail is controlled by the number of *pixels* (picture elements) in a horizontal scan line multiplied by the number of scan lines in a frame. The combined pixel and line count in an image represents what is known as the *spatial density resolution*, or how many total pixels make up one frame. Analog NTSC video is 640 pixels per line with 480 lines. For NTSC digital video, the image resolution was increased to 720 pixels per line with 486 active scan lines per frame.

Increasing the number of pixels in an image increases the amount of detail. This corresponds to an increase in the resolution of the image. If the displayed image is kept at the same size, an increase in resolution would increase the detail in the image. Alternately, a higher resolution image could be displayed much larger while keeping the same degree of detail as the lower resolution image.

For example, if a 720 × 486 image is displayed on a 21-inch monitor, and the resolution of that image is increased, the image would have more detail. Alternately, the same image with increased resolution could be displayed on a larger monitor with no loss of detail.

Aspect Ratios

Video images are generally displayed in a rectangular shape. To describe the particular shape of an image, the width of the image is divided by its height to come up with its *aspect ratio*. This ratio describes the shape of the image independent of its size or resolution. To determine the aspect ratio of an image, the width is divided by the height. For example, a 12 inch by 9 inch image would have an aspect ratio of 1.33 to 1, determined by dividing 12 by 9. Another image of a different size, say 22 inches by 16.5 inches, would also have an aspect ratio of 1.33 to 1, determined by dividing 22 by 16.5. An aspect ratio can be written several different ways. For example, the 1.33 to 1 aspect ratio can also be shown as 1.33:1, 4:3, or 4 × 3 (Figure 12.2).

Pixel Aspect Ratio

The *pixel aspect ratio* is the size and shape of the pixel itself. In computer displays, pixels are square with an aspect ratio of 1 to 1. NTSC pixels have an aspect ratio of 0.91:1, which makes them tall and thin. When setting the standard for digitizing the NTSC video image, the desire was to digitize the image at the highest practical resolution. While the number of pixels in a horizontal scan line could be set to any amount, the number of scan lines could not be arbitrarily increased since they are part of the NTSC standard. Therefore, the pixels were changed to a narrow rectangular shape, allowing an increase in the number of pixels per line and added image resolution.

Figure 12.2 Aspect Ratios

Interlace and Progressive Scan Modes

Interlace scanning is the process of splitting a frame of video into two fields. One field of video contains the odd lines of information while the other contains the even lines of the scanned image. When played back, the two fields are interlaced together to form one complete frame of video.

Where television uses an interlace scanning process, the computer uses a non-interlaced or *progressive scanning* technique. Computer image screens can be refreshed as rapidly as 72 times a second. Because this rate is faster than the persistence of vision, the problem of flicker is eliminated. Therefore, there is no need to split the frame into two fields. Instead, the image is scanned from top to bottom, line by line, without using an interlacing process. The complete frame is captured or reproduced with each scan of the image (Figure 12.3).

Progressively scanned images have about fifty percent greater apparent clarity of detail than an equivalent interlaced image. The progressively scanned image holds a complete frame of video, whereas an interlaced frame contains images from two moments in time, each at half the resolution of the full frame.

The computer industry has always insisted on a far more detailed and higher quality image than has been used in the television industry. Computer images usually require very fine detail and often a great deal of text that would be unreadable on a standard television screen. Present television images do not require the same degree of detail as computer information. In a digital environment, the limiting factor is enough bandwidth to transmit the information. Interlace scanning allows more information to be transmitted in the limited spectrum of space allotted for transmission of signals.

When listing the criteria for a particular standard, the indication of whether the scanning mode is interlaced or progressive appears as an "i" or "p" following the line count, such as 480p, 720p, 1080i, and so on.

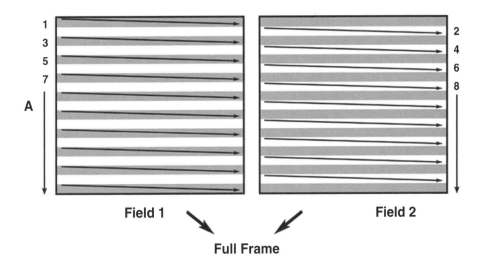

Field 1   Field 2

Full Frame

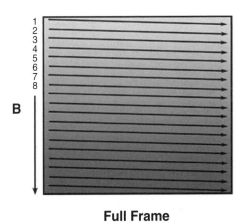

Full Frame

Figure 12.3 A, Interlaced Scanning and **B**, Progressive Scanning

Frame Rate

The frame rate, regardless of the pixel or line count, is the number of full frames scanned per second. This rate represents what is known as the *temporal resolution* of the image, or how fast or slow the image is being scanned. Frame rates vary depending on the rate at which the image was captured or created, the needs or capability of the system using the video image, and the capability of the system reproducing the image.

For example, an image may have been captured at 24 frames per second (fps), edited at 29.97 fps, and reproduced at 30 fps. Each change in the frame rate would denote a different standard. Different frame rates include 23.98, 24, 25, 29.97, 30, 59.94, and 60 fps. Before color was added to the NTSC signal, black and white video was scanned at 30 frames per second, or 30 fps. When color was added to the signal, the scanning rate had to be slowed down slightly to 29.97 fps to accommodate the additional color information.

Standards Categories

Each domain, analog and digital, has its own standards that have a unique combination of factors, such as pixel count, frame rate, and scanning mode. There are two primary categories that embody the analog and digital domains. They are Conventional Definition Television (CDTV) and Digital Television (DTV). Within the DTV category, there are two subcategories, Standard Definition Television (SDTV) and High Definition Television (HDTV).

Conventional Definition Television (CDTV)

When digital video standards were created, the ATSC redefined the prior standards that were already in use. The analog standards used throughout the world were placed in a newly defined category called Conventional Definition Television, or CDTV. CDTV refers to all the original analog television standards.

In the NTSC system, the CDTV standard image resolution is 640 pixels by 480 lines of active video. The frame rate is 29.97 frames per second with two interlaced fields, each containing 240 lines of active video. The PAL standard image resolution is 760 pixels by 580 lines. The PAL frame rate is 25 fps with two interlaced fields, each containing 238 lines of active video. SECAM also has 760 pixels per line and 580 lines, as does PAL, and the two share the same frame rate and scan mode as well.

In the original analog standards, each individual standard contained its own method for processing color information. With the advent of digital video standards, the ISO redefined color encoding to a new international standard called CCIR 601, named after the French organization Comité Consultatif International des Radiocommunications that first developed the standard. Further refinement of the color encoding process also led to a change in name from CCIR 601 to ITU-R 601, named after the International Telecommunications Union.

CDTV Standards	pixels per line	aspect ratio	line count	frame rate	scan mode
NTSC	640	4×3	480	29.97	interlace
PAL	760	4×3	580	25	interlace
SECAM	760	4×3	580	25	interlace

Digital Television Standards (DTV)

The Digital Television category, or DTV, developed out of the growth of the digital video domain. The DTV category encompasses all digital video standards. Its two subcategories, Standard

Definition Television (SDTV) and High Definition Telelvision (HDTV), further divide the DTV category.

High Definition Television (HDTV)

The original HDTV standards were analog because at the time there was no digital television system in use. With the advent of digital, HDTV immediately crossed over into the digital domain. In the process, the quality of the image was vastly improved. There are several different HDTV standards. In addition, many HDTV formats were developed as various manufacturers and various countries began to develop their own standards. The differences between HDTV standards include such elements as frame rate, scan lines, and pixel count. Additional information and specific HDTV standards are discussed further in Chapter 13, High Definition Video.

Standard Definition Television (SDTV)

Not all digital video standards fall into the category of HDTV. Those that have less picture information due to a lower pixel count, line count, or smaller aspect ratio fall under the category of Standard Definition Television, or SDTV. SDTV is the digital equivalent of the original analog standards. It is, therefore, not a high definition image. When a CDTV signal is transferred to the digital domain, it becomes an SDTV signal within the DTV category.

In SDTV, there is a slight increase in the pixel count from CDTV. For example, 640 × 480 NTSC analog becomes 720 × 480 in SDTV, and PAL and SECAM analog signals become 760 × 580 when they are converted to a digital signal. The SDTV category contains standards that use either interlace or progressive scan modes, as well as different frame rates. The aspect ratio for SDTV is 4:3. There are some digital cameras that crop the 4:3 image so it can appear as a 16:9 aspect ratio. But it is simply cropping pixels from view, not adding pixels to increase the aspect ratio. Consequently, it remains standard definition (SDTV), and is not high definition.

Digital Audio

In digital standards, the frame rate for audio need not be the same as the video frame rate. For example, if the rate for video is set at 24 fps, the audio could be recorded at thirty frames per second. There would be no synchronizing problems as long as the 24/30 ratio was maintained. Refer to Chapter 19, Audio for Video, for additional information.

CHAPTER 13
High Definition Video

As noted in Chapter 12, there are two subcategories that fall under the DTV (Digital Television) category of standards, SDTV (Standard Definition Television) and HDTV (High Definition Television). All high definition video, also referred to as high def or HD, falls under the HDTV category of standards. There are several different high def standards, each with its own unique combination of image criteria, including frame rate, pixel count, line count, and scanning mode. While HDTV standards currently represent the highest quality of video image, they are not new standards. In fact, the development of high definition standards began in the analog domain in the early 1970s. Once DTV was developed, HDTV became a digital standard. It currently makes use of the most advanced digital processes.

One of the reasons high definition video was developed was to create a universal world standard. Analog television standards, including NTSC, PAL, SECAM, and variations of these standards, are not compatible with each other. To convert images from one standard to another requires a process that can degrade the image quality. HDTV standards represent an international effort to create more compatibility between world standards. While removing some of the boundaries, high def created an entirely new set of standards that are still evolving.

Widescreen Aspect Ratio

CDTV and SDTV standards use an image size with an aspect ratio of 4 × 3. A 4 × 3 image is four units wide by three units high. While rectangular in shape, it is much closer to a square than the wide-screen image currently seen in cinemas. The human eye perceives a great deal of motion and depth information from the area *outside* of direct view. This area is known as peripheral vision. Having a wider video image area takes advantage of this characteristic and improves the sense of reality for the viewer.

As HDTV was developed, this fact was taken into consideration and all HDTV standards were widened to a 16 × 9 aspect ratio, or an image that is nine units high by sixteen units wide (Figure 13.1). Since the HDTV standards all have a 16 × 9 ratio, it is often referred to as the *native* aspect ratio for the standard. A native standard is the basic standard for which the piece of equipment was designed. It may be capable of handling other standards, but its original intent is called the native standard.

Widescreen video can be played back on a 4 × 3 monitor in different ways. To see the entire widescreen image, the image must be re-duced in size so the width of the image fits on the 4 × 3 monitor. This creates black above and below the widescreen image, a layout often referred to as letterbox. To make use of the full 4 × 3 image area, the sides of the widescreen image can be cropped to show just the middle portion, or 4 × 3 area. Also, a process of panning, or moving horizontally across an image, can be applied during transfer to reveal a particular portion of the widescreen image. This process is often called *pan and scan* (Figure 13.2).

Image Resolution

With the 16 × 9 aspect ratio, there is a larger image area and therefore more room for additional pixels. Different high def stand-ards have different pixel and line counts that make up that standard's image area. The greater the number of pixels there are that make up the image, the greater the image resolution.

For example, one high def standard has an image resolution of 1920 × 1080. In this standard, there are 1920 pixels across one line and 1080 lines in one frame of the image. The 1920 pixel count is the

16 x 9

4 x 3

Figure 13.1

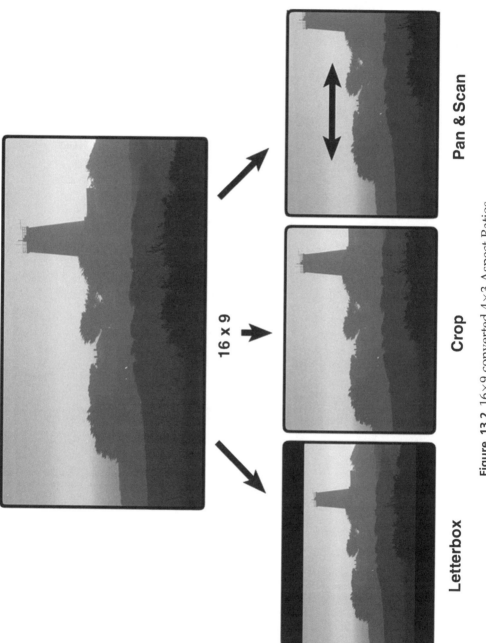

Figure 13.2 16×9 converted 4×3 Aspect Ratios

horizontal resolution, and the 1080 line count is the *vertical resolution.* Another high def standard is 1280 × 720, which is 1280 pixels per line by 720 lines. The combined pixel and line count make up the spatial density resolution of the high def image.

Progressively Segmented Frames

HDTV standards use either one of the two scanning modes, interlace or progressive.

When a high def standard uses an interlace mode, the odd fields are transmitted first, followed by the even fields, just as they are in CDTV or SDTV. In progressive scanning, the entire image is scanned as one complete frame. This data may then be transmitted as a complete frame and received as a complete frame. If there is insufficient bandwidth to transmit the complete frame, the data may be segmented and transmitted in two parts.

Because progressively scanned images are complete frames of video, they require more bandwidth to transmit than may be available. To transmit these images within an interlace environment using narrower bandwidths, a process of segmenting progressively scanned frames was developed.

To do this, the image is divided into two fields by scanning every other line as in interlace scanning. The difference is that in the interlace scanning process, the two fields are from different instances in time. When a progressively scanned image is segmented, the two fields are from the same instant in time. When the separate fields are recombined, the result is a complete progressively scanned frame (Figure 13.3).

This process accommodates the need to segment the data without compromising the quality of the image. Images that are progressively scanned and then transmitted as segmented frames are referred to as *PsF,* for *progressively segmented frames.*

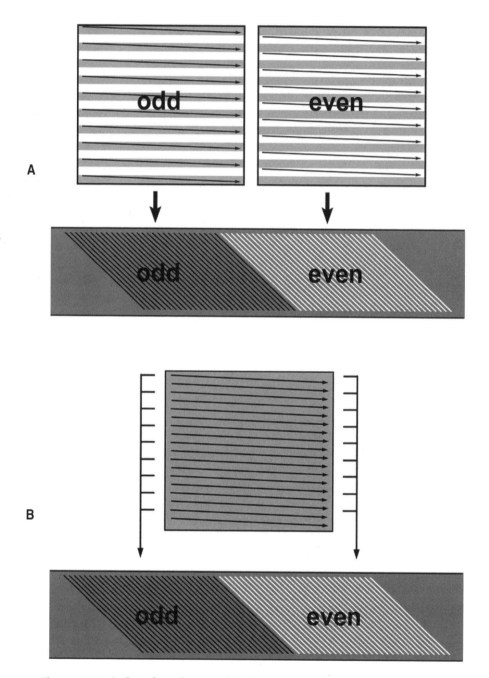

Figure 13.3 **A**, Interlace Scan and **B**, Progressive Segmented Frame

Frame Rate

Within the HDTV set of standards, there are numerous frame rates. The frame rates are part of a set of criteria that defines a particular HDTV standard. Each set of criteria was defined because of specific requirements within an existing physical environment. For example, North American electrical systems use 60-cycle alternating current, while European electrical systems use 50-cycle alternating current.

In addition, one of the major forms of image creation has been film. Film runs at 24fps in North America and 25fps in Europe. To minimize the difficulty in incorporating film into HDTV, a set of criteria was developed to accommodate the film frame rate. A different HDTV standard was created with a specific set of criteria based on the ease with which the new standard would interface with an existing system. Therefore, two of the many HDTV standards include 24fps and 25fps.

Film-to-Tape Conversion

There are many situations when film is transferred to HDTV, or HDTV to film. Film is often used as an archive medium because the film standard has not changed in generations. When film is used as the originating medium, but the delivery requirement is video, film must go through a conversion process. In PAL systems, the existing video frame rate matches the 25fps film rate, and the conversion process is simply a matter of converting from one medium to the other.

However, in the NTSC system, where the video frame rate of 30fps does not match the film rate of 24fps, a different conversion process must take place. In order to smoothly convert or transfer 24fps from film to 30fps in video, a film frame is transferred to video fields. The pattern of this transfer maps four film frames to every five video frames, or ten video fields. The first film frame, referred to as the A frame, is transferred, or pulled down, to two video fields. The second film frame, or the B frame, is transferred to the next three consecutive video fields. The third film frame, the C frame, is transferred to the next two consecutive video frames. And the fourth film frame, the D frame, is transferred to the next three consecutive video frames (Figure 13.4).

The resulting transfer process yields five video frames for every four film frames. Video frame 1 and video frame 2 are each derived from two separate film frames, A and B. Video frame 3, however, is a composite of one field from film frame B and one field from film frame C. Video frame 4 is also a composite composed of one field from film frame C and one field from film frame D. Video frame 5 is composed of two fields, both from film frame D.

When scanning through video images that have been transferred from film using this process, the video frames that contain two different film frames will appear as a double image. When these frames are viewed in motion, however, the double image is not discernable.

When editing video that has been transferred from film using this pulldown process, the sequence of frames must be maintained. If the sequence of video frames is broken, for example by editing two combination frames consecutively, the resulting conflict of images will be discernable when displayed in motion.

This process works well when transferring 24fps film to 30fps video. When transferring film to video running at 29.97fps interlaced, an adjustment in transfer speed needs to be made. To match the timing of the film frames to the video frames at this rate, the film speed must be maintained at 23.976fps, also referred to as 23.98fps. At this speed, the film frames and time sequence will match the video perfectly. Therefore, another HDTV standard contains 23.98fps as part of its criteria.

HDTV Worldwide Standards

The variables of the different HDTV criteria, including all the spatial and temporal resolution options, are what give HDTV its many

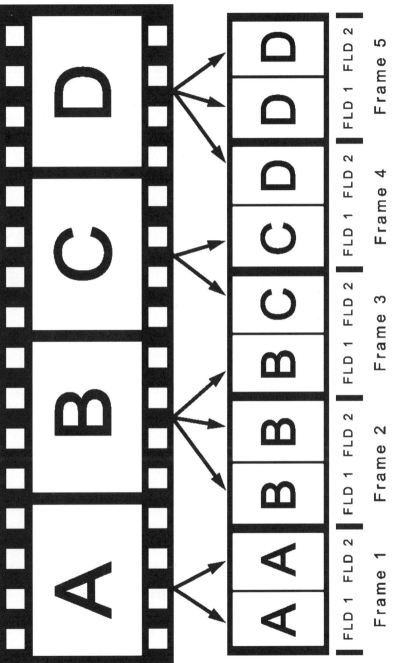

Figure 13.4 2:3 Pulldown

Common Name	# of Pixels / Lines	Aspect Ratio	Frame Rate	Scan Type
24p (1080)	1920 × 1080	16×9	23.98 frames per second[*]	Progressive
1080i	1920 × 1080	16×9	29.97 frames per second[**]	Interlace
720p	1280 × 720	16×9	59.94 frames per second	Progressive
25p	1920 × 1080	16×9	25 frames per second	Progressive

[*]23.98p is also used to refer to 24 frames per second.
[**]29.97p is also used to refer to 30 frames per second.

standards. When referring to HDTV standards, the scan mode is often associated with the frame rate. For example, 24P represents a standard that records and plays at 24fps using the progressive scan mode, whereas 60i represents a standard that records and plays at 60 fields a second using the interlace scan mode. When an "i" for interlace follows a frame rate number, it generally represents the number of fields being scanned, not the frames.

Notice in the table above that there are some standards that differ only by whether the image is scanned using the interlace mode or the progressive mode. Other standards differ in their frame rates, or temporal resolution. And of course others differ in their image, or spatial resolution.

Converting an HD Signal

One of the primary differences between HDTV and SDTV is the increase in the amount of information that makes up the HDTV signal. Because of the number of pixels per line, lines per frame, and frames per second, HDTV has a greater spatial and temporal resolution. While the size of the image is larger and the resolution is greater, the recording, storage, and transmission processes remain similar. Because of these similarities, HDTV signals may be converted to other standards.

Converting HDTV to SDTV or CDTV is referred to as a *downconverting*. In the downconversion process, the number of lines and the number of pixels per line are reduced to fit the targeted standard. For example, a HDTV image that is 1920 × 1080 could be reduced to a 720 × 480 SDTV image. The reduction is achieved by deleting some lines and pixels in the downconversion process. The consequence of this is a reduction in image resolution, though the aspect ratio may remain the same. However, in some situations when a 16 × 9 image is reduced to 4 × 3, the 4 × 3 image may appear as though it had greater detail than the original.

Downconversion is used when an HDTV native image needs to be used in an SDTV or CDTV environment. For example, a program can be shot in HDTV, but transmitted or broadcast in SDTV or even CDTV. Also, if the editing process is configured with SDTV or CDTV equipment, a downconversion from HDTV allows the editing to occur within the existing post-production environment. Some HD VCRs are even equipped to downconvert a signal internally (Figure 13.5).

CDTV or SDTV can also be converted to an HDTV standard through a process called *upconverting*. The upconversion process increases the number of lines and the number of pixels per line to fit the targeted standard. This involves, in some instances, duplication of information to fill in the additional spatial resolution. This does not increase the detail in the image nor the apparent resolution. It merely increases the pixel and line count.

Figure 13.5 Down Converter on HD VCR

Upconversion is used when taking a CDTV or SDTV image and enlarging it to fit in an HDTV space. For example, an older television program that originated in CDTV may be upconverted to HDTV or SDTV for current broadcast. Some equipment contain a downconversion/upconversion circuit within the machine itself. In other cases, the conversion process is accomplished through an outboard or stand-alone device.

HDTV Applications

Because of the different HDTV scanning types and frame rates, HDTV images may look different with each standard. A faster scan rate, or temporal resolution, typical of interlace scanning, gives more frequent image information because it scans an image twice for each frame, once for the odd lines and again for the even lines. The scans are created in different moments in time. This process refreshes the image more frequently than progressive scanning. Therefore, interlace scanning is often used for images that contain a great detail of motion with a lot of action. For example, football games are often shot using 60-field interlace (60i) HDTV. The more frequent scanning of the image fields produces a greater number of images in a given amount of time, creating a smoother transition from field to field and frame to frame.

An HDTV image shot in 24P, or 24fps progressive scanning, gives a less frequent scanning rate or slower temporal resolution. Shooting in 24P means it takes longer to scan a full frame because successive lines must be scanned. A 24P frame rate creates a softer, film-like look. In 24P, rapid motion is not advisable because the slower temporal resolution cannot capture enough motion detail to track the action clearly.

One of the reasons 24P was developed as a standard was to match 35mm motion picture film, both in terms of temporal and spatial resolution. Certain television programs that originated in video are converted to HDTV for archival and sometimes broadcast purposes. However, shows that were created after the advent of HDTV, but during the time HDTV standards were still being defined, turned to film for production purposes. This allowed the shows to be both archived in film, an established medium, and converted to any video standard at a later date.

CHAPTER 14

Digital Scopes

The digital signal differs from the analog signal in several ways, which will be discussed in this chapter. Because of the differences between these two signals, the appearance of a digital scope is quite different from that of an analog scope.

Digital Signal

While the digital signal, as with analog, is 1 volt peak-to-peak, some of the components and measurements within that 1 volt are displayed and measured differently on a digital scope. One volt is divided into a thousand units, each referred to as a millivolt, expressed as mV (Figure 14.1). On the graticule, 1 volt of digital video is displayed from −.3 volts (or −300 mV) to a peak of .7 volts (or 700 mV) for a total of 1 volt. Active digital video is displayed between the 0 base line on the graticule and .7 volts. This relates to 100% video, or 100 IRE units on an analog waveform monitor.

Since the digital signal is a stream of digital information, it does not require the synchronization elements that an analog signal does. Because synchronization is not present in the signal, the face of the scope or graticule, and the measurement of the digital signal, do not contain the synchronizing elements. When a signal is displayed on a digital waveform monitor, there is no horizontal or vertical sync display within the signal (Figure 14.2). On a vectorscope, there is no synchronizing color burst, which normally appears in the nine o'clock position on the vectorscope graticule.

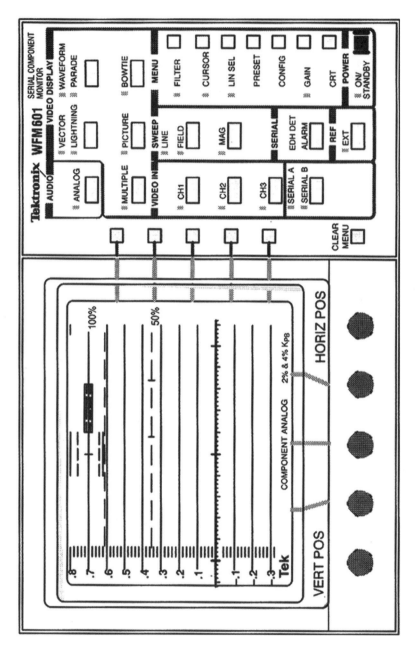

Figure 14.1 Digital Waveform Monitor

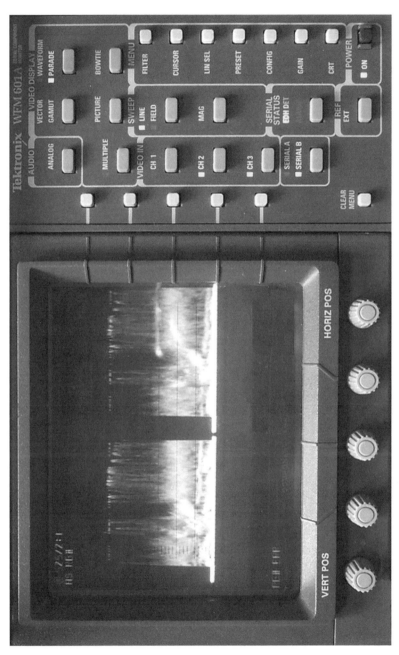

Figure 14.2 Digital Signal Without Sync

While analog black is displayed at 7.5 IRE units, true black in a digital signal is 0, and is therefore displayed at the baseline on the graticule. Because the analog transmission system was designed to put out peak power at the lower video levels, if the analog black signal were true black, or 0 units, the analog signal would electrically overload the transmitter. As a digital signal is a stream of data or digital bits, the levels do not vary over time, but instead remain constant. As a result, digital video can utilize the full range between true black and full luminance.

When measuring analog video, the 75% color bar display is often used so as not to exceed the measuring capabilities of the waveform monitor. A digital waveform monitor is capable of receiving the digital video signal and reducing it to fit within its measuring capabilities. The maximum digital video level is measured at .7 volts, or 700 mV.

Dual Digital Scope Overview

There are several makes and models of digital scopes. For the purposes of this chapter, the Tektronix WFM601 will be used for reference. The WFM601 is a dual-purpose scope that displays both waveform and vectorscope readouts for measuring digital signals. The scope is divided into multiple categories and each of these categories has several buttons. Each button allows several choices (see Figure 14.2). To maximize the use of the scope, some of the buttons are "soft" buttons—their operation changes with a change in menus. One button can perform several different functions depending on the menu selected.

WFM601 Monitor Overview

On the left side of the WFM601 scope is the graticule. Below the graticule are adjustment knobs for the vertical and horizontal positions of the display. The three knobs in the center, with lines pointing to each of them, are adjustment knobs for different options that can be accessed through the menu buttons.

Unlike the older analog scopes marked in IRE units, the scale on the graticule of the 601 scope is marked in millivolts (mV) and ranges from $-300\,mV$ to $+800\,mV$, with each major division being further subdivided into five minor divisions, each one representing 20 millivolts. The horizontal reference line, or base line, is the heavy line at 0 with three large vertical markings between the $-.1$ and $.1$ lines. This line is alternately referred to as the 0% line, $0\,mV$, zero line, blanking level, and black level.

In the middle of the scope, just to the right of the graticule, are five buttons in a vertical line with a Clear Menu button beneath them. These are "soft" buttons that are used to activate the settings that appear next to them. The right side of the scope contains eight sections with the following labels: AUDIO, VIDEO DISPLAY, VIDEO IN, SWEEP, MENU, SERIAL, REF, AND POWER.

Video Display

In the VIDEO DISPLAY section in Figure 14.2, there are buttons labeled WAVEFORM, VECTORSCOPE, LIGHTNING, PARADE, MULTIPLE, PICTURE, and BOWTIE. These buttons are used to select the type of display that will appear on the CRT. The waveform and vectorscope displays are similar to analog scopes. The other displays were created to examine color and luminance information in a digital environment where no sync or subcarrier signals exist.

The LIGHTNING display compares the color difference signals (P_BP_R) with the luminance signal (Y). It is best used when varying the levels of the luminance and color difference components. This is discussed further in Chapter 21, Test Signals, Displays, and Media Problems.

On an analog waveform CRT, the signal can be viewed as luminance only (LOW PASS), chrominance only, or flat, which is the combination of both luminance and chrominance. On a digital scope, these signals can be combined into one display called PARADE. When PARADE is selected, the CRT displays the luminance signal (Y) and both color difference signals (P_BP_R) (Figure 14.3).

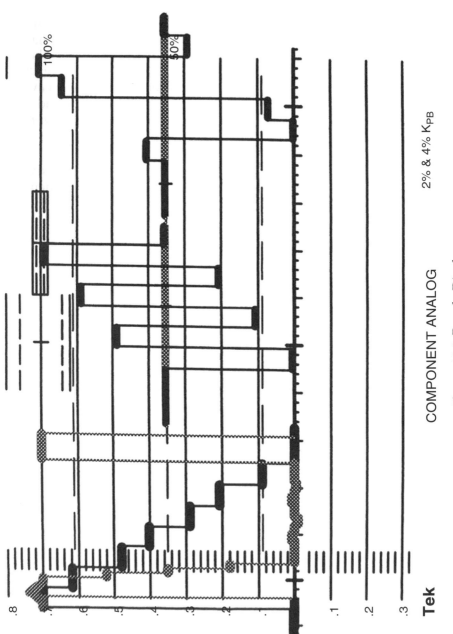

Figure 14.3 Parade Display

The MULTIPLE display allows more than one signal to be viewed simultaneously. When WAVEFORM or PARADE is selected, it is possible to add a Vector (vectorscope), LIGHTNING, or DIAMOND display. The Diamond display is discussed in Chapter 21.

When PICTURE is selected, the CRT displays a monochrome version of the video signal from the digital input. Whatever image is coming from the digital source can be viewed in this display. This display is used to verify the incoming source.

The BOWTIE display is used to compare the timing and gain or amplitude of the color difference signals to the luminance signal. This is discussed further in Chapter 21.

Video In

Under the section called VIDEO IN are CH 1, CH 2, and CH 3 buttons. These buttons represent the luminance and chrominance signals. CH 1 is Y or R, CH 2 is P_B or G, and CH 3 is P_R or B. These three channels of information can be turned on or off. However, at least one channel remains on at all times.

Some display signals, such as BOWTIE, display specific channels. For example, the left waveform in the Bowtie display compares CH 1 to CH 2. The right waveform always compares CH 1 to CH 3.

The SERIAL A/B button selects the "A Input" or the "B Input" of the scope. What signal is input will vary from facility to facility.

Sweep

Like an analog waveform monitor, the SWEEP selection chooses between a horizontal line display and a vertical field display. The LINE and FIELD buttons toggle through two different positions each. The LINE button will display both a 5 μs/division and a 10 μs/division. The FIELD button will display either a one-field display of information or a two-field display.

The MAG button turns on the horizontal sweep magnifier to display the information in 1 µs/division in a two-line sweep rate, or .5 µs/division in a one-line sweep rate, or in the 25X magnification for both the one- and two-field sweep rates.

Reference

The REFERENCE (REF) button selects either the internal serial digital reference or an external video input for the scope's reference. If the scope is being used to measure signals from an output device, it is recommended that the scope's reference be locked to that device. If for some reason a reference is not available, the scope can be locked to its own internal reference.

Menu Section

Under the MENU section are options for FILTER, CURSOR, LIN SEL, and GAIN menus. This group of menus expands the measuring capabilities of the selections under VIDEO DISPLAY and SWEEP. They are identified by LED indicators to the left of each function when that particular function is selected. Only the menu readout for the last function selected will be displayed, even though more than one menu item may be chosen.

Also under the MENU section you will find the PRESET button, which allows the recall of nine different presets that can be stored, plus one factory setting. Each of the presets can be assigned a unique set of parameters. These might include line blanking, horizontal or vertical blanking, closed captioning measurements, and so on.

The CONFIG button brings up six separate submenus that allow measurements of the signal in different configurations. The CRT button brings up a menu used to control the CRT display, i.e., FOCUS, SCALE, INTENSITY, READOUT INTENSITY, and TRACE ROTATION. When these menus appear, the soft buttons to the right of the graticule and the soft knobs below the graticule will change functions depending on the menu selected.

CHAPTER 15

Compression

Compression is the process of reducing data in a digital signal by eliminating redundant information. This process reduces the amount of bandwidth required to transmit the data and the amount of storage space required to store it. Any type of digital data can be compressed. Reducing the required bandwidth permits more data to be transmitted at one time.

Compression can be divided into two categories: *lossless* and *lossy*. In lossless compression, the restored image is an exact duplicate of the original with no loss of data. In lossy compression, the restored image is an approximation, not an exact duplicate, of the original.

Lossless Compression

Lossless compression is characterized by a complete restoration of all the original data that was contained in the original image. Compressing a document is a form of lossless compression in that the restored document must be exactly the same as the original. It cannot be an approximation. In the visual world, lossless compression lends itself to images that contain large quantities of repeated information, for example, an image that contains a large area of one color, perhaps a blue sky. Computer-generated images or flat colored areas that do not contain much detail, e.g., cartoons, graphics, and 3D animation, also lend themselves to lossless compression.

One type of lossless compression commonly used in graphics and computer-generated images (CGI) is *run-length encoding.* These images tend to have large portions using the same colors or repeated patterns. Every pixel in a digital image is composed of the three component colors, red, green, and blue, and every pixel has a specific value for each color. Therefore, it takes three bytes of information, one byte for each color, to represent a pixel.

Run-length encoding, rather than storing the RGB value for each individual pixel, groups each scan line into sections, or run-lengths, of identical pixel values. For example, one section of a line of video might consist of a row of 25 black pixels. This section would be run-length encoded as 25, 0, 0, 0. This translates as 25 pixels, each composed of $R = 0$, $G = 0$, and $B = 0$, or black. The original image would have required 75 bytes (25 pixels $\times$ 3 bytes) to hold this data. When compressed using run-length encoding, the same data can be contained in four bytes.

Lossy Compression

Video images generated by a camera are generally not suited for lossless compression techniques. Rarely are there long enough run lengths of the same pixel value in an image to maximize the efficiency of these techniques. Compression used for active video is usually in the *lossy* category. With lossy compression, the restored image will be an approximation of the original. When a lossy image is reproduced or uncompressed, not all the data left out during compression will be restored exactly as they were.

To minimize the apparent loss of data, lossy compression techniques generally compress the data that comprise those parts of the image the human eye is less sensitive to, or that contain less critical image data. The human eye is more sensitive to changes in light levels or luminance than it is to changes in color, both hue and saturation. Within the color gamut, the human eye is more sensitive to the yellow-green-blue range. The human eye is also more sensitive to objects in motion than to still objects. Rabbits, for example, will freeze when they are in the presence of a predator. They know instinctively that the eyes of a predator animal, which includes humans, are more sensitive to objects in motion. Therefore, the rabbits are less likely to be seen while remaining motionless.

In lossy compression, the data chosen to be compressed is the data that does not fall within the human sensitivity range or data that contains a great deal of motion. Two commonly used lossy compression techniques are JPEG and MPEG. These techniques, and variations of them, are described below.

JPEG Compression

JPEG compression was developed by the Joint Photographic Experts Group and defines the standards for compressing still images, such as graphics and photographs. In JPEG compression, the image data is separated into luminance and chrominance information. JPEG takes advantage of the human eye's greater sensitivity to changes in luminance than changes in color by sampling the chroma or color information in the image half as often as the luminance. In this manner, the chrominance data is reduced by half. The total data can be reduced further by encoding redundant luminance information in the image. Any constant values that appear in the image can be encoded using the same run-length technique used in lossless compression.

Motion JPEG Compression

Motion JPEG, or M-JPEG, was developed from JPEG as a means of compressing moving images by treating each image as a single still picture. Only incremental changes are necessary between adjacent frames of video, as the quantifiable difference from frame-to-frame tends to be less than 5%. Treating each image as a single still rather than as part of continuous motion is an effective approach to compressing motion images.

MPEG Compression

MPEG compression was developed by the Motion Picture Experts Group and defines the standards for compressing moving images. MPEG techniques establish the protocols for compressing, encoding, and decoding the data but not the encoding methods themselves. The rules dictate the order of the data and what the data must contain but not the method by which the data is derived. This allows for continuous improvement in encoding techniques without having to constantly change existing equipment. As in M-JPEG compression, MPEG takes maximum advantage of the interframe similarity as the key to its compression techniques.

MPEG-1

Each line within each field of digital video contains 704 pixels. MPEG-1 compression uses 1 field per frame of video sampled at 352 pixels per line. Using half resolution horizontally and every other scan line vertically creates a quarter-resolution image. MPEG-1 is the simplest form of motion compression. There is no detailed analysis of each individual image or adjacent images. Consequently, no advantage is taken of redundant information that occurs within each frame and between adjacent frames. It is compression based on a simple, mathematical progression of sampling every other pixel on every other line.

MPEG Variations

MPEG-2 compression can use a variety of computer algorithms, or mathematical formulas, to compress the images. These different algorithms are referred to as *tools,* and can be used in combination to provide progressively more compression without loss of quality. In other words, MPEG-2 compression can produce a good quality image using about 4% of the original video data. In addition, MPEG-2 is flexible and can support a wide variety of data rates, picture sizes, and compression qualities.

Each successive variation of MPEG compression, e.g., MPEG 4, 5, 7, and so on, is more sophisticated in its ability to discern compressible data, allowing for increased compression without degrading the image. Different MPEG compression techniques or variations can lend themselves to specific applications.

The MPEG Process

The MPEG process starts by analyzing a sequence of video frames known as the video stream. Redundant information is encoded and compressed. The compressed video stream is then encoded into a *bit stream*. The bit stream is then stored or transmitted. The speed with which the data is processed is called the *bit rate*. The data is decoded and uncompressed when it is to be used and the image restored to its original form.

MPEG compression utilizes a combination of two different compression schemes, *spatial* and *temporal*. Spatial compression reduces the quantity of data contained in each frame of video by eliminating the redundant data within the image. Temporal compression compares the changes between the images over time and stores the data that represents only the changes. Spatial compression uses the same technique as JPEG compression, described above, to create an *intra picture,* called an *I frame.* Unlike the temporal compression frames, the I frames are complete "stand-alone" images that can be decoded and displayed without reference to any surrounding frames.

The I frames are interspersed within the video stream and act as references for the temporal compression between frames. The arrangement is somewhat like a picket fence, with the I frames representing the relatively few fence posts while the temporal frames are the many pickets. The temporal compression frames, called *B* and *P* frames, contain motion information that describes how the different regions of the I frame have changed between the intervening frames. The B and P frames contain far less data than the I frames. They contain only the data about the changes that have occurred between frames. This accounts for the great efficiency of MPEG encoding. Compression rates of 25:1 can be achieved with little or no noticeable degradation in the quality of the uncompressed image. I frames and B and P frames are described in more detail below.

I Frames

An *I frame* (Intra picture) is one frame that is a complete image sampled in detail so it can be used as a reference for the frames around it. Each I frame is divided into 8 × 8-pixel blocks. These pixel blocks are placed in groups of 16 × 16 called *macroblocks*, which are then compressed using JPEG compression techniques. I frames are created as often as needed and particularly when there is a substantial change in the image content. Typically in a video stream, this occurs approximately two times per second.

P Frames

The frames before and after the I frame, labeled P and B, contain the data of the changes that occur between themselves and the I frame. *P frames* (Predictive pictures) contain descriptions of how the pixel blocks in the previous frame have changed to create the current frame. These descriptions of distance and direction of movement are called *motion vectors*. The decoding process for the current frame looks backward at the previous frame and repositions the pixels based on the P frame motion vectors. The previous frame could be either an I frame or another P frame. If there is a change in luminance or color, that difference is also encoded with the motion vector.

If there is a substantial change in the image, new pixel blocks are created for the portion of the image that has changed. These new blocks are derived from the source video and use the same encoding method as the I frame. P frames cannot stand alone or be directly accessed since they are dependent upon the information in the previous frames from which they are derived. P frames contain much less data than I frames and are therefore simpler to encode.

B Frames

B frames (Bidirectional pictures) are similar to P frames in that they are made up of motion vectors and picture blocks. The difference is that they look both forward *and* backward to compare pixel blocks, where the P frames only look backward to the previous frame.

When new elements enter the picture, the pixels in a B frame can be compared forward *or* backward to pixel blocks in either I or P frames. The difference between the previous and following frames is the data used to create the B frame.

The B and P frames both consist of data that reflect only the changes between the frames and not data about the complete image itself. For this reason, neither B nor P frames can stand alone as single images.

The Group of Pictures (GOP)

I, B, and P frames are grouped together to form a *Group of Pictures,* or *GOP.* A GOP must start and end with an I frame to permit its use as a reference for the surrounding B and P frames. A GOP can contain just P frames or both B and P frames in between the I frames. The number of B frames or P frames within a GOP can be increased or decreased depending on image content or the application for which the compressed video is intended. For example, a fast-moving action sequence with complex content (lots of detail) would use shorter groups, hence more I frames. Group lengths typically range from 8 to 24 frames. The following shows the typical GOP structure for 30 frames of IBP-encoded video stream:

IP Method

Excellent compression quality can be achieved using just I and P frames, even though the P frames only use backward references in time. The following example shows three frames of the source video material encoded only with I and P frames (Figure 15.1).

The source video material (top row) shows a truck moving left to right over a city background.

The compression process starts with an I frame, which is a JPEG compression of a single frame of video.

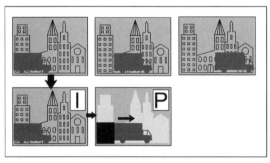

In the next step, a P frame is generated that refers backward in the sequence of images to the previous I frame. The P frame contains motion vectors that describe the position of the background and the movement of the truck. when the truck is repositioned, the area of the background that is uncovered leaves a "hole" in the background (black square).

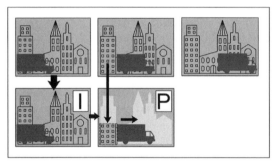

To fill in the missing part of the background, blocks of pixels are copied from the I frame using JPEG compression and combined with the motion vector data contained in the P frame.

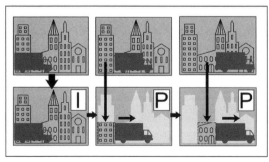

The procedure is repeated for subsequent P frames which refer back to the previous P frame, retrieve data from the I frame, and fill in any new "holes".

Figure 15.1 IP Method of Compression

IBP Method

The addition of the optional B frame increases the compression quality and lowers the rate of data transmission. The B frame looks both forward and backward in time so the frame with the most helpful information can be used as a reference (Figure 15.2).

Bit Rates

From the point of view of data compression, the complexity of an image is determined by the combination of the amount of movement or change from frame to frame and the quantity of detail contained in the image. To maintain proper image motion in time, the zeros and ones, or digital bits, that comprise the data must be transmitted and received quickly enough to reproduce the image. Depending on the complexity of the image and the required level of quality, different data rates, or *bit rates*, are used.

If the images are less complex in nature, or if the required level of quality is not high, a fixed data rate or bit rate may be used. Where the images are either more complex or the required level of quality is high, variable bit rates may be used in order to maintain a reduced data rate while not compromising the quality.

Variable Bit Rates

Although video runs at a fixed frame rate, the amount of data required to encode each frame can be variable, depending on scene complexity. Variable bit rates allow for consistent picture quality when the complexity of the image varies. Each part of the image is analyzed and compressed at its optimal compression rate. Less complex portions of the image are compressed at higher rates while more complex portions of the image are compressed at lower rates. In order to achieve variable bit rates, there must be greater analysis of the image content to achieve the best quality with the least amount of data. With variable bit rates, the encoding process is more complex and cannot be done in real time.

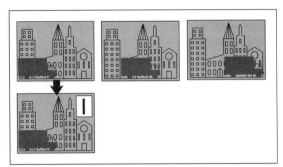

Like the IP method, the IBP method starts with an I frame.

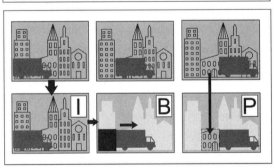

In the next step, the last frame of GOP is generated as a P frame first. The P frame refers back to the I frame with motion vectors to describe the background and the movement of the truck. A again, any "holes" in the background are filled in with pixel blocks from the I frame.

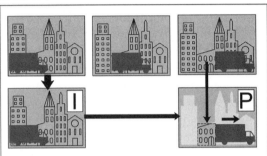

The B frame is then generated by motion vectors for the objects in motion. Like the IP method, the truck's movement uncovers a region of the background leaving a "hole" in the picture.

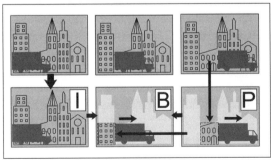

The B frame is completed by filling in its "holes" with pixel blocks from either the I or P frames by looking both forward and backward in time.

Figure 15.2 IBP Method of Compression

Fixed Bit Rates

Fixed bit rates result in varying levels of picture quality because there is no allowance for image complexity. Broadcast media, such as cable, satellite, and terrestrial broadcasting, require fixed bit rates for their transmission equipment. Live broadcasts, satellite linkups, and playback of uncompressed video all require real-time compression before being transmitted. Fixed bit rates can be used to compress images in real time, whereas variable bit rates cannot.

Profiles and Levels

The I, B, and P tools can be combined into progressively more sophisticated compression techniques called *profiles*. Picture quality can improve depending on the profile used. Each profile can be divided into *levels* of quality, depending on the compression tools used and the physical parameters of the compressed video, such as the picture size, resolution, and bit rates. There are four levels that provide a range of picture quality, from limited definition (1/4-resolution video) to high definition with 1080 scan lines. Each level has its own specific standard for the input video, such as Standard Definition video or High Definition video.

Main Profile at Main Level

The different profiles and levels can be mixed and matched to create a wide variety of picture sizes, bit rates, and encoding qualities. The most useful combination is the *Main Profile at Main Level* (abbreviated as *MP@ML*). Main Profile means that I, B, and P frames can be used for compression and Main Level means that the picture resolution is 720 × 480 in NTSC. Different storage and delivery systems have different bit rate constraints. The I, B, P compression tools are flexible enough that MP@ML can adjust the bit rates. Lowering the bit rate reduces the picture quality unless it is compensated for by using more sophisticated encoding tools.

Bit rate	Application
2 Mbits/sec	Equivalent to VHS quality
4 Mbits/sec	NTSC/PAL broadcast quality
10 Mbits/sec	DVD quality
15 Mbits/sec	Equivalent to DV quality

Various bit rates for Main Profile at Main Level

	Pixels	1	2	3	4
scan line 1	Y	X	X	X	X
	R-Y	X		X	
4:2:2 sample	B-Y	X		X	
scan line 2	Y	X	X	X	X
	R-Y	X		X	
4:2:2 sample	B-Y	X		X	

4:2:2 sampling across each scan line of video

Video Encoding and Compression

After converting RGB video signals into luminance and chrominance data, the chrominance portion can be compressed with little apparent loss in image quality. The RGB channels are converted into luminance (Y) and two chrominance channels (R-Y and B-Y).

The above table illustrates the digitizing scheme for 4:2:2 video. For every set of four pixels on a scan line, there are four digital samples of the luminance channel. Only two samples are taken for each of the two chrominance channels. Each chrominance sample is *shared* by two pixels. As a result, the two chrominance channels are digitized at half the resolution of the luminance channel, reducing

	Pixels	1	2	3	4
scan line 1	Y	X	X	X	X
	R-Y	X		X	
4:2:2 sample	B-Y	X		X	
scan line 2	Y	X	X	X	X
	R-Y				
4:0:0 sample	B-Y				

4:2:0 sampling alternates between 4:2:2 and 4:0:0 on each scan line

the amount of data for those two channels by 50%. This reduces the total data required for each frame of video by 33%.

4:2:0 sampling takes the idea of undersampling the chrominance channels a step further than 4:2:2. If, for every four pixels, there were four samples of luminance but no samples of chrominance, that would be 4:0:0 sampling. Of course, with no chrominance data you would only have a black and white picture. However, if every other scan line was digitized at 4:2:2 and the lines in-between were digitized at 4:0:0, the chrominance data from the 4:2:2 scan lines could be shared by the alternating 4:0:0 scan lines, further reducing the amount of data required to describe a frame of video.

The table above illustrates how 4:2:0 sampling alternates between 4:2:2 and 4:0:0 sampling on each scan line. Each chrominance sample is therefore shared by two pixels horizontally as well as two scan lines vertically. This means that the chrominance samples cover a 2 × 2 area, or four pixels. As a result, the two chrominance channels each have only 25% of the data that the luminance channel has. Reducing the data requirements for two channels to 25% reduces the total data required for each frame of video by 50%.

Compression Artifacts

The compression and decompression process introduces small errors into the restored image or the audio signal. When these errors become noticeable, they are called *artifacts*. The type of artifact depends on the type of compression used and the signal content.

Chrominance smear—As a result of low luminance levels or high chroma levels, colors can bleed across sites on a chip. The result is called *smearing*. The appearance is that of colors blending between areas in the image.

Chrominance crawl—Very fine vertical stripes in a scene can produce high frequency luminance signals that start to be interpreted as chrominance information. This appears as a shimmer of rainbow colors over the striped surface.

Blocking—the appearance of small, regular squares that appear to *tile* an entire still image.

Mosquitoes—fuzzy dots that can appear around sharp edges after video compression.

Bit starvation (audio compression)—a harsh or gritty sound, loss of detail, and less pronounced separation.

CHAPTER 16
Magnetic Media

All video images begin as a form of light, which is then converted to electrical signals. These electrical signals can then be converted to either a magnetic or optical signal for purposes of recording or storage. The two primary methods used to record or store video are magnetic recording, as in videotape, or optical recording, as in DVDs. This chapter will deal with magnetic recording and media.

Magnetic Recording

Magnetic media is based on the physics principle that electricity, or electrical signals from a converted light source, that passes through a wire, creates a *magnetic field* around the wire. If that wire is wrapped around a soft iron core, that iron core will become an *electromagnet* (Figure 16.1). The process can be reversed. A magnetized iron core moving in a coil of wire can be used to create an electrical current in the coil of wire.

The iron core is bent in the shape of a circle where the ends do not touch. Touching both ends together would complete the energy flow and the iron core could not be used to magnetize the tape. Therefore, a gap or space is left between the two poles. This gap is a small opening that is visible under high magnification. By leaving this gap, the flow of magnetic energy follows the path of least resistance, which is to the tape. The coating on the tape has greater permeability and therefore provides an easier path than trying to cross the gap between the two ends of the magnet. The magnetic energy deposits itself on the tape and is stored there.

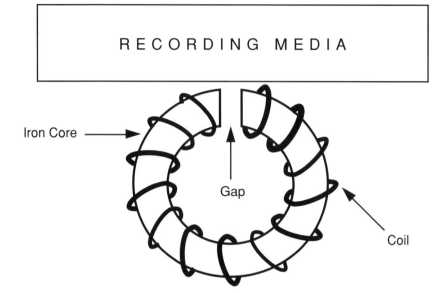

Figure 16.1 Coils of Wire Around an Iron Core

On a magnetic recording device, such as a videotape recorder, there is a record *head,* which is the part of the machine that records the signal (Figure 16.2). This record head contains a coil of wire wrapped around a soft core of iron. The video or sound signals are converted to electrical energy. When this electrical energy flows through the coil of wire in the record head, it causes the record head to become a magnet. The strength of the magnetic field varies depending on the amount of electricity that is flowing through the coil of wire around it.

As the tape passes across the head, the varying magnetic energy levels, called *flux,* magnetize the particles on the surface of the tape. The amount of electricity, and thus the magnetic energy, varies depending on the strength of the signal. The signal represents both the amplitude and frequency of the data being recorded. The levels of magnetic energy are analogous to the variations in the signal. The particles on the tape do not move. Instead, these little particles of metal act as small magnets. As magnets, they retain their magnetic energy until they are either demagnetized through

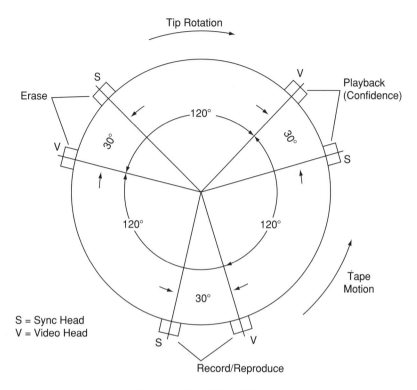

Figure 16.2 Video Heads

erasure, or are altered by replacing the information with newly recorded material.

Two other aspects of the magnetic recording process are important to note. They are *bias* and *equalization*. Magnetic recording media has an initial resistance to being magnetized. This resistance is overcome through a process known as *bias*. Biasing magnetic media allows a very high frequency signal to be recorded, on the order of 100 to 200 kilohertz, at a low energy level. This high frequency signal overcomes the media's resistance to recording the incoming signals. Because this bias signal is so high in frequency, it is undetectable and causes no interference. The media is now more easily magnetized by the incoming signals about to be recorded.

Playing back the tape is the reverse of the recording process. The tape, which is magnetized, is passed across the playback head, that part of the machine that converts the magnetic energy back to electrical energy. The varying magnetic energy levels cause electrical current to flow in the coil of wire that is wrapped around the soft iron core in the playback head. Varying levels of electrical energy based on the strength of the magnetic energy are produced in the coil of wire. This electrical energy is then amplified and reproduced as the information that was originally recorded.

Magnetic media, specifically videotape, can be used to record either analog or digital signals.

Control Track

When a video signal is recorded onto magnetic media, a *control track* is recorded (Figure 16.3). A control track serves a similar function to perforations in film. If it were not for the perforations in film, there would be no way to place the frame in its proper position in the gate of a projector. The control track aligns the scanner in the VTR, or the

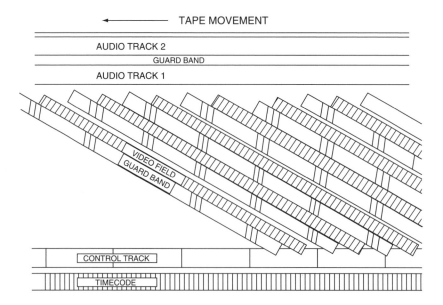

Figure 16.3 1-Inch Videotape Tracks

record/playback head in a floppy or hard drive, so that the playback begins at the start point and finishes at the end of the data track. The scanner or record/playback head aligns itself with the tracks one at a time as it plays them back.

A tape or disk drive that has never been recorded on has no control track. The control track is created as the recording is made. As the head moves across the tape or disk, a control track pulse is formed at the proper time. In a VTR or VCR, there is one control track pulse for each rotation of the video head. When the tape is played back, the heads on the playback machine are aligned in exactly the same way as when the video tracks were recorded.

Signal-to-Noise Ratio

While digital information is not subject to analog noise, the fidelity and clarity of analog recorded data is compromised by the inclusion of noise in the recording. Noise is defined as any electrical or electromagnetic energy that interferes with or distorts the signal or desired data. Noise can be generated by any number of spurious signals that exist in the physical world, e.g., electrical energy, transmitted electro-magnetic radiation, and static electricity. Noise can also be generated by the nature of the recording media.

For example, as a magnetic recording tape passes across a record/ playback head, the friction of the magnetic particles against the metal of the head creates a hiss that is recorded as noise. Because of the minute size of the particles, and the speed of the tape across the head, this hiss or noise tends to be a high frequency. Recorded noise becomes part of the signal, making the noise difficult to identify and remove. In Chapter 20, a process of noise reduction is discussed.

The balance between the signal or desired data and the noise is referred to as the *signal-to-noise ratio*, or *S/N*. The stronger the signal containing the desired data, and the weaker the noise signal, the greater the signal-to-noise ratio. S/N ratios are generally expressed in *decibels (dB)*, a measurement of signal strength. A signal-to-noise ratio of 59 dB would indicate a 59 to 1 ratio of signal information to noise. Because the decibel system of measurement is built using logarithms, this is not as great a difference as it appears. A 59 to 1 ratio does not mean that the signal is 59 times stronger than the noise. For example, a ratio of 10 dB to 1 dB does not indicate an energy level 10 times as great. It is in actuality only twice the energy level.

Magnetic Tape

Magnetic tape is made by grinding a metal oxide into a very fine powder, mixing it with a glue or binder, and coating it on a plastic backing. In the recording process, the metal compound becomes magnetized. To manufacture magnetic tape, a metal compound had to be chosen that was abundant, inexpensive to manufacture, and simple to use. There are only three metals that can be magnetized: iron, nickel, and chrome. The original metal compound chosen was common iron oxide or rust because it fit all the criteria.

Since the development of magnetic tape, many improvements have been made in both the oxides and the backings onto which the oxide is coated. Plain iron oxide has given way to other compounds that have increased the recording tape's ability to hold magnetic energy, giving it a better signal-to-noise ratio. The plastic backings have become thinner, more flexible, and stronger at the same time. With some tapes, the back of the plastic base is coated with a carbon compound to ensure better friction between the tape and drive mechanisms of the record or playback machine.

Computer floppy disk technology uses the same recording principle as magnetic tape. Inside the floppy disk hard shell case, there is a circular, thin, floppy plastic disk that is coated with a metal oxide compound. This metal compound is magnetized in the same manner as tape, with the only difference being that the floppy disk itself moves in a circular motion as opposed to the linear motion of tape.

Metal Tape

An improvement in recording tape was made with the development of pure metal coatings to replace oxide based coatings. The advantages of metal tape are the greatly increased magnetic properties that come with pure metal. In oxide-based recording media, a signal that contains more energy than the magnetic particles on the tape can retain will become saturated. This causes distortion or loss of data in two ways. First, saturation occurs when the signal is so strong that the magnetic energy bleeds across into adjacent particles, thereby destroying that data. Second, some of the signal energy or data may not even be recorded as the metal particles are unable to retain the complete signal.

A pure metal tape will not saturate as easily. A stronger signal can be recorded without danger of distortion. The ability of the coating to hold more magnetic energy means greater signal strength in the S/N ratio, more information on a smaller quantity of tape, and better retention of the magnetic information over longer periods of time.

However, pure metal coatings were not used originally because they were too coarse and too abrasive. This type of coating would have caused excessive wear on the record/playback heads and greatly increased the high frequency noise that is created as the tape passes across the heads. The pure metal coating also had poor adhesion to the plastic backings.

In order to use pure metal coatings, a process was developed for encapsulating the metal particles so they did not cause friction as they pass across the heads. The encapsulation process created a barrier between the metal particles and the machine. The barrier does not affect the magnetic properties of the metal, but does keep the metal particles from contacting the heads. This prevents excessive head wear and noise. The encapsulation process helps the metal adhere to the plastic backing.

Modulation and Demodulation in Analog Recording

Modulating a carrier frequency is the method used to transmit a broadcast signal. When transmitting a television signal, video is transmitted in the form of an amplitude-modulated carrier. The audio signal is transmitted as a frequency-modulated carrier.

When recording video, it is also necessary to use a modulated carrier. The amount of information that is contained in a video signal is more than can be recorded on tape. To facilitate recording, video signals are recorded as a frequency-modulated carrier. Audio signals are direct recordings and are not modulated. Direct recording means that the signal is recorded in its full spectrum and not compressed as a modulated carrier.

In playback, the recorded video signal is demodulated, the carrier is filtered out, and the information that was stored on the carrier is reproduced as a video image. As audio is a direct recording, there is no demodulation necessary when playing from tape.

Erasing Media

Erasing any magnetic media, either analog or digital, can be achieved in two ways. First, the media can be bulk erased. Bulk erasing requires putting the media into an electromagnet, or *degausser*. In a degausser, a strong magnetic field is created in which either the media is rotated or the magnet is rotated. During the process of rotation, the media is physically moved away from the magnet and the magnetic field is reduced in strength. This drains the magnetic energy from the media. Magnetic energy still remains, but because it is low in intensity and scrambled, the media appear to be blank.

The degaussing process can also take place while a VTR is recording. When a VTR begins recording, an erase head is turned on. The erase head emits a strong magnetic field. As the tape moves across the erase head, the existing magnetic energy is replaced by a high frequency, high energy random signal. The record head then records the new desired magnetic signals on the tape.

On magnetic media, such as a floppy disk, when data is deleted, it is not actually erased. It is simply flagged as available disk space for the next recording process. This is why computer files are capable of being retrieved even after they have been marked for deletion. When new data is about to be recorded, an erase head is activated that deletes the old data. A record head then records the new data.

Hard Drives and Servers

Digital data, when converted to magnetic energy, can be recorded on a hard drive. A *hard drive* is a magnetic disk storage device made of steel onto which the digital data is recorded. Recording occurs through a record head, similar in construction and type to a tape-based recording device. The record head consists of a soft iron core enclosed in a coil of wire. It is mounted on a movable mechanical arm that allows the head to be brought into close proximity without touching the disk surface. As the disk rotates at high speed, the record head magnetizes the disk surface on whatever part of the disk is flagged as available space. As the arm moves up and down depositing data on the disk, it emits an audible clicking noise.

Hard drive storage capacity can be increased by grouping a series of disks together as a unit. In this manner, the storage capacity of a hard disk-based system can be virtually unlimited. As the data on any magnetic media are volatile, duplication of data on an array of disks can prevent accidental loss. This type of redundancy is referred to as a *RAID* system, a *Redundant Array of Independent Disks*. There are several varieties of RAIDs providing various levels of protection.

Centralized groups of hard drives, or storage systems, can be used to provide data for a variety of users simultaneously. These storage systems are called *servers*. Servers come in many forms, from simple twin hard drive units to complex groups containing hundreds of disks, and they have a variety of uses. For example, once news footage is loaded onto a server, access to that footage would be available to reporters and editors worldwide, the instant it was recorded on the servers' disks. The data can be copied, changed, and stored separately by multiple users without affecting the original data, thereby providing speed and flexibility to the users.

Magnetic Formats

There are different formats of magnetic recording devices. The most commonly used tape devices are videotape recorders (VTRs) or videocassette recorders (VCRs). A tape format identifies the tape size and method of recording video and audio signals. There are open reel and cassette formats, and professional as well as consumer formats. As formats have developed, the video and audio quality has improved, and in most cases, the tapes and the machines that play them have decreased in size and cost. Below is a listing of some of the tape formats currently in use. All are cassette formats except 1-inch tape, which is an open reel format. Timecode, which is referred to below, is a labeling system recorded along with the audio and video signals. Timecode is discussed in detail in Chapter 18.

1-inch—An analog composite tape format still in use. The tape is 1 inch in width. The video is recorded through the process of frequency modulation of a carrier. The audio is limited to two channels and is a direct recording. Timecode is recorded on a separate channel (Figure 16.4).

BetacamSP—An analog component format. It includes four channels of audio. However, two of the four channels are embedded in the video information. Two of the audio channels are directly available while the two embedded channels can only be recorded simultaneously along with the video signal. Timecode is recorded on a separate dedicated track.

Digital Betacam—Evolved from the Betacam SP VCR, some models are capable of playing back both the digital Betacam tapes as well as the older analog Betacam tapes. However, the format can only accept a digital input and record a digital signal. Digital Betacam uses a digital component recording process for video.

Figure 16.4 1-Inch VTR

The format includes four separate and distinct audio channels. Timecode is recorded on a separate dedicated track. There is also a separate analog cue track that is used for locating specific audio portions of the recording. As a digital format, it uses a compression process that compresses at approximately a 3:1 ratio with a sampling rate of 4:2:2 (Figure 16.5).

D2—A digital composite format referred to as "anything in, anything out," meaning that it can accept analog or digital inputs, and can output analog or digital signals. There are four separate and distinct audio channels. Timecode is recorded on a

Figure 16.5 Digital Betacam VTR

separate dedicated track, and there is also a separate analog audio cue track.

D5—A high definition recording format that is component digital. It has four discrete audio channels, a separate timecode track, and a separate analog audio cue track. Being a high definition machine, it has the capability of recording and playing back several of the existing high definition standards. It is capable of recording an uncompressed video signal. It can also record compressed data at a 4:1 compression ratio. This format can play back and record at different frame rates.

D7 or DVC-PRO—A digital component format. It has a compression ratio of 5:1, with a 4:1:1 sampling rate. It has two separate audio channels and a separate analog audio cue track. Timecode is recorded on a separate track. The D7 format comprises several variations: the DVC-PRO; DVC-PRO50, which uses a 4:2:2 sampling rate; the DVC-PROP, which is a progressive scan using a 4:2:0 sampling rate; and the DVC-PROHD, which is the high definition version of the format.

DVCAM—A digital component format using a 5:1 compression ratio. It uses a 4:1:1 sampling rate for a 525/60 NTSC source or a 4:2:0 signal for a 625/50 PAL source. Audio can be recorded either as a two-channel or four-channel signal, depending on the audio sampling rate. The format has provisions for recording timecode. However, it is not broadcast compatible. The timecode used in this format is proprietary to the manufacturer. The format does not have a separate audio cue track. DVCAM VCRs will play back both DVCAM and the DV format cassettes.

HDCAM—A digital component high definition format that uses a 4:1 compression and 4:2:2 sampling rate. There are four separate audio channels, an analog cue track, and a separate timecode track. The format can record both high definition and standard definition signals, and is "digital only" for both input and output. This format can play back and record at different frame rates (Figure 16.6).

Figure 16.6 High Definition VTR

CHAPTER 17
Optical Media

The digital video signal can be stored magnetically or optically. Optical media is a development of the digital domain. It is not used for analog recording or storage, only for recording or storing digital data. The primary difference between magnetic and optical media is that magnetic media are volatile, meaning that the information can be lost accidentally by exposure to a strong magnetic field. Optical media, on the other hand, are non-volatile. The data, once recorded, cannot be changed or erased except through direct action by the user.

Optical Recording

All optical media use laser technology for recording, storing, and reproducing digital data. There are three primary components of a laser system: a laser, a lens, and the recording media.

Ordinary light, such as a light bulb, is referred to as *incoherent light.* Incoherent light is composed of multiple frequencies that are scattered in all directions. A laser is an optical device that generates *coherent light* in the form of a beam (Figure 17.1). Coherent light has a single, specific frequency. A laser beam is created when electrical current is used to energize or excite a chemical compound. Specific chemicals emit specific frequencies of light. Therefore, a laser beam is a single, specific frequency of coherent light.

This light is then focused through a lens, which may be made of a variety of transparent materials. Industrial-grade rubies are

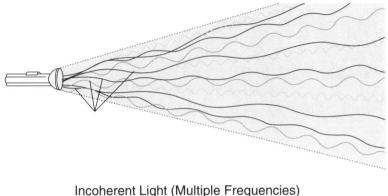

Incoherent Light (Multiple Frequencies)

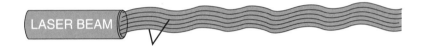

Coherent Light (Single Frequency)

Figure 17.1 Laser Beam

often used as the lens material, accounting for the red color of common lasers. Light energy used in the creation of an image or acoustical energy used in the creation of sound is converted to electrical energy, which is then used to energize the laser. Electrical energy turns the laser on or off depending on whether it is being energized by a zero or one, as described below.

The recording media is generally in the form of plastic that creates the base into which the laser beam burns the digital data. The laser beam melts the plastic in a series of pits as it is turned off and on. The pits register as zeros. Areas where no pits are burned remain flat and register as ones. These pits and flats are recorded in a circular track starting from the inside, or center of the disk, going outward toward the edge (Figure 17.2). The process is slightly different when CDs or DVDs are created by consumers on home equipment.

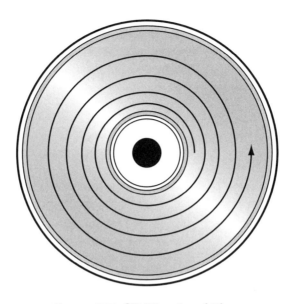

Figure 17.2 CD Directional Flow

Optical Reproduction

In order to read the pits and flats from the plastic recording media, a reflective surface is required. Aluminum, which can appear as silver or gold, is generally used as the reflective backing against the plastic (Figure 17.3). The aluminum backing also protects the digital data on the plastic from being damaged.

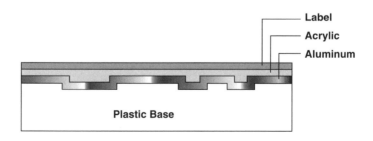

Figure 17.3 CD Cross Section

When reproducing or playing back the data, the laser beam remains on constantly. The constant light shining on the surface of the disk is reflected back by the aluminum backing. The system interprets the difference in time between a reflection off a flat surface and a reflection off a pit. This difference in time allows the system to read the information as zeros or ones.

Optical Formats

The principal difference among optical formats is how much data can be stored on a single disk. While the flow of digital data is measured in bits, all digital memory is measured in bytes. A high-speed internet connection is measured as so many *bits per second (bps)*, whereas a single sided device such as a CD can hold between 700 and 800 MB, or MegaBytes, of data.

The hierarchy of measurement is as follows: A *kilo* equals one thousand. *Mega* equals one thousand kilos, or one million. *Giga* equals a thousand megs, or a thousand million, which is a billion. *Terra* equals a thousand gigs, or a thousand billion, which is a trillion. *Peta* equals a thousand terras, which is a thousand trillion, or a quadrillion. When referring to digital memory, shortcuts are used and capitalized, such as KB for kilobytes, MB for megabytes, GB for gigabytes, and so on. Lower case shortcuts are used in reference to bits of data, such as Kb for kilobits, Mb for megabits, Gb for gigabits, and so on.

CDs and DVDs are the same type of optical media. The difference between the two formats is one of storage capacity. Storage capacity on optical media is a function of the number of tracks that can be stored or written on the surface of the media. DVD development grew out of a desire to store more data. By making the tracks on the disk narrower and placing them closer together, a greater storage capacity became available. Physically, CDs and DVDs are the same size. However, a single-sided DVD, which has a memory of approximately 4.7 GB, can store more than six times the information that a CD can.

Primarily, CDs are used for audio recording, still images, and, to a limited degree, motion. Recording of images in motion is limited on CDs only because of the quantity of memory available on the disk. DVDs, because of a greater storage capacity, are often used for recording images in motion, such as movies, games, and interactive video.

Unlike CDs, which are only single-sided devices, DVDs are available in different formats. Some DVDs are single-sided, single-layered devices and some can be double-sided and double-layered. Single-layered DVDs have a storage capacity of 4.7 GB, while double-sided, double-layered DVDs can store as much as 17 GB of data. A 17 GB DVD can hold up to 8 hours of video using MPEG-2 compression. The MPEG-2 compression process used for DVDs is generally built on a 40:1 compression ratio.

While there are erasable and re-recordable versions of both CDs and DVDs, they are, for the most part, ROM or Read Only Memory devices. ROM memory is not volatile and not meant to be easily erased. ROM memory is designed for permanent storage, which is why it is Read Only Memory. Blank CDs and DVDs, meant to be recorded on by the consumer, are denoted by the letter R, e.g., CD-R, DVD-R. In addition, there are versions of CDs and DVDs that, after the initial recording, can be erased and rewritten. These are denoted with the letters RW, e.g., CD-RW, DVD-RW.

Fiber Optics

While fiber optics cannot be used to record or store digital media, they are increasingly used to transmit digital signals. Fiber optics makes use of lasers and light pulses in a manner similar to CDs and DVDs. Electrical energy is converted into pulses of light that travel through a glass fiber that is the fiber optic cable. Rather than the laser beam burning a pit or leaving a flat on the plastic disk, it transmits light through the cable. A light pulse represents a one, and no light represents a zero.

There are two modes of fiber optics: single-mode and multimode. *Single-mode* fiber optics uses only one frequency of light to transmit the data through the fiber optic cable. However, multiple streams of serial digital data can be grouped together and transmitted simultaneously through the single fiber. This process is known as *multiplexing*. Multiplexing exploits the spaces that occur between packets of data to insert additional data. In this way, many data streams can be interwoven and sent simultaneously.

Multimode fiber optics uses multiple frequencies of light simultaneously to carry multiple streams of data (Figure 17.4). Each light frequency can be multiplexed to carry several streams of data. The multiple light frequencies can then be combined and transmitted through the fiber optic cable. Multimode fibers are capable of carrying more data than single-mode fibers.

Single-mode fiber is capable of carrying digital data up to 5 kilometers, or about 3 miles, before the light pulses need to be reamplified to continue transmission. Multimode fiber is capable of carrying digital data up to 3 kilometers, or approximately 1.8 miles, before the light pulses must be reamplified. Over a long distance, the cost of building reamplification facilities adds dramatically to the cost of using multimode fiber.

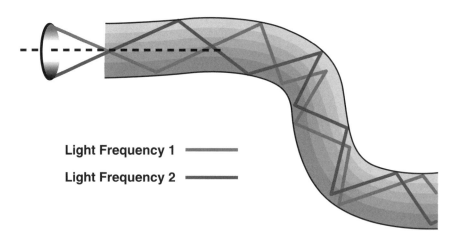

Light Frequency 1
Light Frequency 2

Figure 17.4 Multimode Fiber Optics

Fiber optics promises to greatly expand the possibilities of digital data transmission. For example, in a 3-year period, the data transmission capabilities went from 1 Gb per second to 1000 Gb per second, a thousand-fold increase.

Magneto-Optical Systems

Magneto-optical systems make use of both magnetic recording and lasers for data storage purposes. In a magnetic-optical system, the laser is used to heat the magnetic media to more readily accept the digital data. This allows for higher speed of recording and faster retrieval.

CHAPTER 18
Timecode

In the early days of broadcast television, all programs were broadcast live. The only means of archiving a television program was by using a process called kinescope. Kinescoping was the process of focusing a 16 mm motion picture camera at a television monitor and photographing the images. The shutter was adjusted to accommodate 30 fps of video, though the film ran at 24 fps.

Starting in the mid-1950s, when videotape recording was invented, programs were taped live and then played back for broadcast at a different time. These programs were played in real time without the benefit of instant replays or freeze frames. When videotape began to be used for editing purposes, it became critical to identify specific frames of video, access those frames, then cue and edit them to specific locations in an edited master tape. Film frames traditionally could be identified by numbers imprinted along the edge of the film. At the time of manufacture, video had no numbering that could be used to identify individual video frames.

In the 1950s, SMPTE (Society of Motion Picture and Television Engineers) created timecode, a system by which videotape could be synchronized, cued, identified, and controlled. SMPTE timecode records a unique number on each frame of video (Figure 18.1). Working with time-coded video ensures that a specific video frame can be accessed using the same timecode number over and over again with complete accuracy. This is often referred to as frame accuracy, as in having a frame-accurate editing system or making a frame-accurate edit.

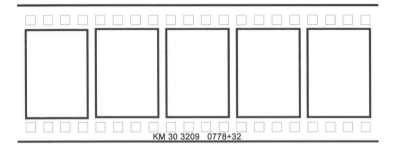

FILM FRAMES LABELED WITH EDGE NUMBERS

| 2:29:35:16 | 2:29:35:17 | 2:29:35:18 | 2:29:35:19 |

VIDEOTAPE WITH TIMECODE LABELING EACH FRAME

Figure 18.1 Labeling Frames

Reading Timecode

Timecode is read as a digital display much like the clock displays used in sporting events. However, in addition to the hours, minutes, and seconds of a digital clock, timecode includes a frame count so the specific video frames can be identified and accessed. A timecode number is displayed with a colon separating each category, constructed as follows:

00:	00:	00:	00:
hours	minutes	seconds	frames

A timecode number of one hour, twenty minutes, and three frames would be written as 01:20:00:03. The zeros preceding the first digit do not affect the number and are often omitted when entering timecode numbers in editing systems or other equipment. However, the minutes, seconds, and frames categories must use zeros, as they hold specific place values.

Here are some examples of how timecode is read and notated:

2:13:11	Two minutes, thirteen seconds, and eleven frames.
23:04	Twenty-three seconds and four frames.
10:02:00	Ten minutes, two seconds, and zero frames. (It is necessary to hold the frames place even though its value is zero. If the last two zeros were left out, the value of this number would change to ten seconds and two frames.)
3:00:00:00	Three hours even.
14:00:12:29	Fourteen hours, twelve seconds, and twenty-nine frames.
15:59:29	Fifteen minutes, fifty-nine seconds, and twenty-nine frames.

Timecode uses military clock time in that it runs from 00:00:00:00 to 23:59:59:29, that is, from midnight to the frame before midnight. In a 30-frames-per-second standard, if one frame is added to this last number, the number turns over to all zeros again, or midnight. The frame count of a 30 fps video is represented by the 30 numbers between 00 and 29. The number 29 would be the highest value of frames in that system. Add one frame to 29, and the frame count goes to zeros while the seconds increase by 1. The frame count of a 24 fps video is represented by the 24 numbers between 00 and 23.

Timecode can be used with any available video standard regardless of that standard's frame rate. The only difference in the timecode numbering process is that the last two digits indicating frames may appear differently. The frames will reflect whatever frame rate was chosen as the recording format. For example, a timecode location in a 24 fps HDTV standard might be 1:03:24:23, which represents the last frame of that second; whereas the last frame of a 30 fps HDTV standard would be 1:03:24:29. Some of these timecodes reflect accurate time, and others do not.

Timecode Formats

Since its development, timecode has had several formats. The original format was *Longitudinal Time Code*, or *LTC*. Longitudinal timecode is recorded as a digital audio signal on a separate audio track. On 1-inch format NTSC VTRs, longitudinal timecode is recorded on track 3, leaving tracks 1 and 2 for program audio. In the PAL and SECAM standards, the timecode for 1-inch VTRs is recorded on track 4.

On many of the videocassette formats, such as Betacam and Digi-Beta, there is a separate audio track reserved specifically for longitudinal timecode. As with the formats mentioned above, this timecode audio track can be recorded, erased, or changed without affecting the existing audio or video signals already on tape. Because LTC is an audio signal, the source media has to be in motion in order for the timecode number to be interpreted correctly. Just as a scream on tape is silent when the tape is in pause, so is timecode that is recorded on an audio track.

Another timecode format is *Vertical Interval Time Code*, or *VITC*, pronounced *vit-see*. While LTC is an audio signal, VITC is recorded as visual digital information in the vertical interval as part of the video signal. VITC must be recorded simultaneously with the video. Once recorded, VITC can be used to identify a frame of video either in still mode or in motion.

There is also a form of timecode used with the $\frac{3}{4}$-inch videocassette format called *address track*. Address track timecode is recorded on a special timecode track that is in the active video area of the tape along with the image. Because of this, address track code cannot be recorded after the fact, but must be recorded along with the video at the time the recording is being made. Because of the placement of the address track timecode in the active video signal, machines not designed to interpret the code will display a disturbance in the video.

Non-Drop Frame and Drop Frame Timecode

When timecode was created, video was still monochromatic and ran at an exact 30 fps. With the advent of color in analog video, the scanning frequency slowed video to 29.97 fps. In other words, it takes more than 1 second to scan a full 30 frames. In fact, it takes 1.03 seconds to scan 30 frames of color video.

The original timecode labeling system still applied, but because of the slower rate of color video, there was a difference between actual clock time and the timecode reference of time. If every color video frame was numbered sequentially with the original 30 fps time-code, at the end of an hour the timecode would read 59 minutes, 56 seconds, and 12 frames, or 3 seconds and 18 frames short of an hour, even though the program ran a full hour. There are fewer frames per second and thus fewer frames in an hour.

Broadcast programs have to be an exact length of time in order to maintain a universal schedule. In order to allow timecode to be used as a reference to clock time for color video, SMPTE created a new method of time coding that made up for the 3 seconds and 18 frames, or 108-frame difference. It was determined that numbers should be dropped from the continuous code by advancing the clock at regular intervals. By doing this, there would be an hour's duration in timecode numbers at the end of an hour's worth of time.

The specific formula SMPTE created began by advancing the clock by two frames of timecode numbers each minute, *except* every tenth minute (10, 20, 30, and so on). By advancing 2 frames on every minute, a total of 120 frames, or 12 more than the 108 frames needed, would be dropped. But 2 frames dropped from every minute *except* the tens of minutes would be 54 minutes × 2 frames per minute, which equals 108 frames, accounting for the necessary amount of frames to identify a true clock time period. SMPTE named the new alternative method of time coding color video *drop frame timecode*, in reference to its process. Drop frame timecode is sometimes referred to as *time of day*, or *TOD*, timecode. The original 30 fps continuous code was subsequently termed *non-drop frame timecode* (Figure 18.2).

In drop frame timecode, the timecode is always advanced by skipping the first two frame numbers of each minute except every tenth minute. For example, the numbering sequence would go from 1:06:59:29 on one frame to 1:07:00:02 on the very next frame (see Figure 18.2). The two frame numbers that are skipped are 1:07:00:00 and 1:07:00:01. At the tenth minute, no numbers are skipped. The numbering sequence at each tenth minute would go from, for example, 1:29:59:29 on one frame to 1:30:00:00 on the next.

A convention is followed when working with timecode numbers that helps to identify whether they represent drop frame or non-drop frame timecode. If the punctuation before the frames value is a semi-colon, such as 1:07:00;00, it is drop frame timecode. If there is a colon dividing the frames, such as 1:07:00:00, it is non-drop frame timecode.

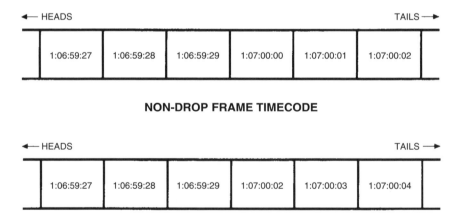

Figure 18.2 Timecode Formats

Like non-drop frame timecode, drop frame timecode leaves no frames of video unlabeled, and no frames of picture information are deleted. The numbers that are skipped do not upset the ascending order that is necessary for some editing systems to read and cue to the timecode. At the end of an hour's worth of material, there will be an hour's duration reflected in the timecode number as well.

Drop frame timecode has been adopted for longer format programs where it is necessary to account for a specific amount of time. Many shorter programs and commercials use non-drop frame timecode because the difference in the frame count is insignificant. For example, a 1-minute commercial will show a 2-frame difference between its actual length and the timecode numbers, if it is using non-drop frame timecode. A 10-minute program will show an 18-frame difference, or a little over a half second. However, a 1-hour program with a 3:18 frame difference would be too big a discrepancy to be tolerated within a broadcast environment.

Timecode Generators and Readers

Timecode is created within a timecode generator. Sometimes, in the case of cameras, an internal timecode generator produces a timecode number that is recorded onto tape. With some higher end cameras, it is possible to set the timecode generator to a specific number so it will generate new timecode starting from that number. Less expensive cameras generally start the coding automatically at 00:00:00:00.

Larger facilities will have external timecode generators with additional features. For example, these generators can not only be set to produce a specific timecode number, but also to read an incoming timecode signal, and then lock on to that signal and regenerate it. This is also referred to as *slaving* the timecode generator to an external source.

The timecode generator can be programmed to produce any time-code number from 00:00:00:00 to 23:59:59:29 in either drop frame or non-drop frame. There is usually a switch or menu option on the generator that can toggle back and forth between the two different modes (Figure 18.3). Once it is set, however, the generator will continue to use that particular frame code mode until it is changed.

Timecode generators are often set to the time of day. If the generator runs free throughout the day, the timecode that is recorded onto tape will always match the time the recording took place. This system can provide a reference for tracking when scenes were captured.

Timecode numbers have to be read and interpreted. This is done through a timecode reader that translates the digital timecode information into visible timecode numbers. A timecode reader may be a stand-alone device or incorporated as part of a group of equipment. The display of the timecode reader is generally an LED or sometimes a fluorescent display.

Visual Timecode

Time code can also be displayed as numbers over the visual images. This is achieved through the use of a character or text generator or sometimes through an internal filter in an editing system. The time-code signal is fed into the character generator, and the character generator in turn displays a visual translation of the timecode numbers. That display is mixed with the video material and can be shown on the monitor or recorded into the picture. Visual time-code is not a signal that can be read by a videotape machine, computer, or timecode reader or generator. It is used as a visual reference for viewing purposes only (Figure 18.4).

Visual timecode can be recorded in different sizes and can be placed anywhere on the video material. It can also be recorded

Figure 18.3 Timecode Generator

Figure 18.4 Visual Timecode

with a background box or mask around the numbers for the highest level of clarity. In most cases, a matte is used because the numbers can be seen clearly no matter what the video background material may be. For example, if there is light-colored background material, white timecode numbers would not show up very well without a darker matte around them.

CHAPTER 19

Audio for Video

Human perception and learning is 90% visual. This creates a greater tolerance in the range of acceptability in visual images. Because audio comprises a much smaller percentage of human information gathering, even a small audio discrepancy will translate into a much greater perceptible difference. Even so, audio was always thought of as less important than video.

People are more critical of what they hear than what they see. It has been found through experimentation and research that people will watch poor-quality images if the audio is good. On the other hand, the audience will not tolerate poor audio because it is more of a strain to make sense of the content. If audio is out of sync by one frame, one thirtieth of a second, it is obvious and annoying. It would be better in those instances if there were no audio at all. In contrast, if the video level is too high or low by a few percentage points, it is not nearly as distracting.

Measuring Volume

Sound is measured in *decibels*, notated as *dB*. The dB measurement was developed many years ago by Bell Laboratories, which was then a division of the Bell Telephone company, hence the measurement in *bels*. The human ear responds to a remarkable range of sound amplitude, or loudness. The difference between the bare perception of audio and the threshold of pain is on the order of a 10 trillion to 1 ratio. Because this range is so enormous, a measuring system had to be created that reduced this range of information to more manageable numbers.

In mathematics, logarithms are often used to simplify large calculations. For example, a logarithm can reduce 10 to 1 ratio to a 2 to 1 ratio. That is, the ratio of 10 to 1 becomes 2 to 1 when measured as a logarithm. Logarithms can be used with any numeric system, such as base 10 or base 2. When logarithms use the decimal system, or base 10, to simplify the measurement of sound, that measurement is referred to as *decibels*. All decibel measurements are logarithmic functions.

The decibel is not a specific measurement like an inch or foot is an exact measurement of distance. A decibel is actually the ratio between a measured signal and a 0 dB reference point. For acoustics or acoustical engineers, the 0 dB reference point is the threshold of hearing. For electronics, the 0 dB reference point is the maximum allowable power for a transmitted audio signal. Therefore, a 0 dB measurement refers to a very different level of sound in acoustics than it does in electronics and a different measuring scale is required.

Acoustic engineers use an acoustic measuring system called *dBSPL*, or decibel sound pressure level. The measurement of acoustic sound is based on air pressure. Electronic audio signals are based on an electrical measuring system. This scale uses a volume unit measurement, or *VU*. The maximum allowable strength for a sustained transmitted audio signal is *0 dBVU*. For analog electronic recording, it is permissible to have analog audio signals that momentarily exceed 0 dBVU by as much as +12 dB.

Digital recording is a serial stream of digital data. Because this digital stream represents every aspect of the audio signal, including frequency and amplitude, increases or decreases in dBVU do not add to the quality of the signal. Digital audio recordings are generally made in the −12 dB range. If a digital audio recording is made at greater than 0 dBVU, there will be distortion and loss of data.

Analog Audio

The audio signal encompasses a much smaller range of spectrum space than video. Because of this, audio recordings in analog are direct recordings. Early analog VTR formats were manufactured with either one or two channels of audio. In order to respond to the demand for additional audio tracks, beyond the capabilities of existing equipment at the time, encoding techniques were developed to increase the number of available audio channels.

One method of encoding used was to interweave the audio into the video tracks during the recording process. By using an FM or frequency modulation encoding process, the audio signal could be recorded along with the video and not interfere with the video portion of the signal. The *audio frequency modulation* process, or *AFM*, was developed by Sony and used in their BetacamSP VCR format. By using the AFM tracks, the number of audio channels on BetaSP recordings was increased from two to four.

A similar method of encoding, called HiFi, was used on consumer VHS, S-VHS, and Hi8 formats to expand the number of audio tracks for those formats. Both AFM and HiFi recordings give greater audio fidelity along with greater frequency and dynamic range.

In AFM and HiFi recordings, the enhanced audio channels or tracks are available if the playback machine has the ability to reproduce them. The standard longitudinal tracks are also available. The only drawback to these enhanced audio channels is that they must be recorded at the same time as the video. Any changes or additions to the AFM channels would require re-recording the video. The longitudinal tracks, however, can be recorded at any time, with or without the video.

With the availability of these audio channels, the recording of additional, discrete audio material was possible. For example, music, dialogue, and sound effects could be recorded onto individual channels for mixing later. The added channels also meant that a *separate audio program*, or *SAP*, could be used for additional languages. For visually impaired consumers, a *DVS* channel, or *descriptive video system*, was developed to verbally describe what is occurring visually on the screen.

Digital Audio

When recording a video signal, the audio portion is included with the video as part of the serial digital stream. A digital audio signal has several benefits. Because noise is analog information, audio recorded as digital data is immune to analog noise problems. Also, as a serial digital stream, digital audio allows for recording and reproducing with a greater dynamic and frequency range.

Since digital audio is in the stream of signal data, no separate audio connections are required. One connection, referred to as SDI (Serial Digital Interface), carries the serial data that includes audio, video, synchronizing, time code, and so on. The number of audio channels is not limited by the equipment or the physical recording process. The only limitation in the number of digital audio channels is the processing speed and the available bandwidth. Like analog, separate channels can be designated for music, effects, dialogue, SAP, DVS, and so on.

Sampling Rates

Harry Nyquist, an American physicist, developed the theorem that sampling of a sine wave had to be slightly more than twice the highest frequency in order to be successfully reproduced. If the sampling rate is equal to or less than the original frequency, data will be lost at certain points along the wave. The reproduced signal will be incomplete (Figure 19.1).

Human beings are sensitive to only certain areas of the frequency spectrum. The ear is capable of hearing between 20 and 20,000 Hz, or 20 kHz (kilohertz). Based on the Nyquist theorem, the sampling rate for audio had to be slightly more than 40 kHz, or 40,000 samples per second. The original sampling rate for audio was set at 44.1 kHz. In the interest of better fidelity in reproduction, the sampling rate was increased to 48 kHz. In certain instances, the sampling rate has been increased to 96 kHz and as high as 192 kHz.

Each sample taken is composed of digital bits. The number of bits contained in the sample can vary. A sample can be composed

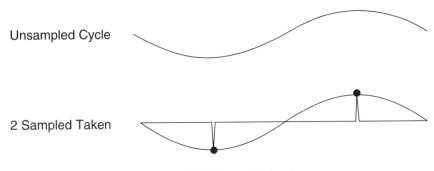

Unsampled Cycle

2 Sampled Taken

Figure 19.1 Nyquist chart

of 8 bits, 16 bits, 20, 24, or 32 bits, and so on. The more bits in the sample, or the larger the digital word used, the truer the reproduction. Both the frequency of sampling and the number of bits contained in the sample are restricted only by the bandwidth and the speed of the equipment creating or reproducing the data.

Audio Compression

Sampling is part of the digitizing process. Audio, like video, once it is digitized or sampled, can be compressed. The compression process reduces the quantity of data by reducing redundant information. Within the range of human hearing—20 Hz to 20 kHz—the range of 2 to 5 kHz, which is the range of the human voice, is most sensitive. During the compression process, this range is given a higher proportion of the compressed audio data stream. Frequencies above and below this range are more heavily compressed and are allotted a smaller percentage of the data stream.

Audio is typically compressed by a factor of about ten to one. As with video compression, there are also different audio compression techniques that are used, depending on the sound quality desired, and the bandwidth and sampling rates available. The MPEG process of compression is the most common. Within the MPEG compression process, there are three data rates that are used. Each of these data rates is referred to as a *layer*.

Layer 1	192 Kbits/sec	Lowest compression
Layer 2	128 Kbits/sec	Medium compression
Layer 3	64 Kbits/sec	Highest compression

A layer is a data transfer rate that is based on the number of samples per second and the number of bits contained in that sample. Each of these layers represents a different quality of reproduction. Each layer is compatible with the layer below it. In other words, Layer 1 can reproduce Layer 2 and Layer 3. Layer 2 can reproduce Layer 3, but they are not backward compatible.

Layer 1 is the lowest rate of compression, thereby yielding the best fidelity of the original signal. The bit rate is 192 Kbits per second, per channel.

Layer 2 is a mid-range rate of compression. The bit rate is 128 Kbits per second per channel. In stereo, the total target rate for both channels combined is 250 Kbits per second. This is the layer used with most MPEG-encoded video.

Layer 3 is the lowest bit rate compression at 64 Kbits/sec per channel. Layer 3 uses complex encoding methods for maximum sound quality at minimum bit rate. This is the standard popularly referred to as *MP3*, which represents MPEG-2 Audio Layer 3.

Audio Formats

The original analog tape formats were reel-to-reel recorders. These evolved into audio cassette decks. An audio cassette is basically a reel-to-reel device except that the reels are enclosed within a cassette casing. Digital audio can be recorded on both magnetic and optical media. Audio devices using magnetic media include floppy disks, mini-disks, and solid-state recording devices such as those used for MP3. Optical recording devices include CDs and DVDs.

The original analog formats recorded audio as a direct, uncompressed signal. Digital formats can record the audio signal as either compressed or uncompressed (full bandwidth). The MPEG process is the most commonly used form of compression.

What You Hear

No matter how sound is recorded, compressed, or reproduced, how it is heard depends on the recording technique that is used. For example, mono audio, also referred to as monophonic or monaural, consists of a single audio signal without reference to left, right, front, or rear. When played back, mono audio imparts no information as to the direction or depth of the sound. Other audio recording systems, such as stereo and surround sound, include data that do impart information as to the direction and depth of the sound.

Stereo Audio

In audio recording, *stereo* is the process of having separate left and right channels. This more closely resembles the way sound is normally heard. Due to the position of the ears on either side of the head, each ear receives the sound at a slightly different time, allowing the brain to locate the source of the sound. With stereo recordings, the sound is separated so that each ear hears the sound in a natural way, lending a sense of depth and reality (Figure 19.2).

Surround Sound

The term *depth* in audio refers to the surroundings in which the audio was recorded. A concert hall has very different audio dynamics than an automobile. To accurately reproduce the sense of sound, direction, and depth from a concert hall, for example, additional audio data must be included in the signal. In addition to left and right stereo, sound must also come from behind the listener on the left and right.

Audio recordings that contain this additional information are called *surround sound*. Surround sound includes left and right

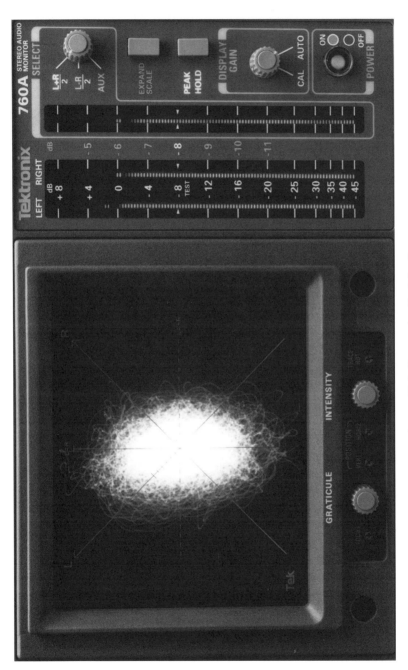

Figure 19.2 Stereo Audio Monitor

channels in front of the listener, left and right channels behind the listener, and a center channel located directly in front of the listener (Figure 19-3). In addition to these five channels, surround sound also includes a *Low Frequency Enhancement* channel, or *LFE*. The LFE adds a greater sense of audio depth and reality by boosting the low frequencies. Because low frequency sound is non-directional in nature, the placement of the LFE speaker is not critical. Surround sound is referred to as a 5.1 audio system. The LFE is represented by the .1 in the 5.1 reference.

Noise Reduction

Any form of analog recording on tape creates an inherent high frequency hiss. This is caused by the movement of the oxide particles across the audio heads while the tape is in motion. The particles rubbing on the audio heads create a hissing sound somewhat like rubbing sandpaper on wood. The noise is created by a physical phenomenon and is not a recorded signal. It is the nature of the recording medium.

A process of noise reduction in analog recordings was developed by Ray Dolby, an engineer who was also involved in the original creation of videotape recording. Dolby discovered the range of frequencies that comprise this high frequency hiss. He determined that by amplifying the high frequencies in the recorded signal, and then attenuating or reducing those signals to their original levels on playback, the high frequency noise inherent in analog tape recordings could be reduced. If the high frequencies were simply reduced on playback without the first step of amplification, the high frequencies in the signal would be lost. Dolby encoding can be used for any type of analog recording on tape.

The original Dolby process, referred to as *Dolby A*, boosts the high frequencies of the audio being recorded. This is known as *Dolby encoding*. When the encoded signal is played back, the boosted high frequency recording is brought back to its original state. This is referred to as *Dolby decoding*. Because the high frequencies in the audio signal have been amplified to match the inherent tape hiss,

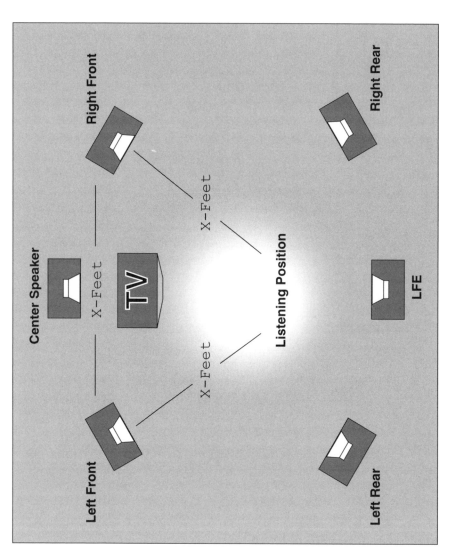

Figure 19.3 Surround Sound

the noise level is reduced during decoding. Reducing the noise level makes the noise inaudible when listening to the audio playback.

There have been further improvements made in the Dolby process, increasing its ability to reduce noise. *Dolby B* and *Dolby C* were improvements made in consumer formats, with C being a further improvement over B. The two are compatible in that Dolby C machines can decode Dolby B recordings. The processes are essentially the same as Dolby A.

Dolby SR (spectral recording) is another improvement in professional formats. The SR process boosts the mid-range frequencies as well as the high frequencies for better noise reduction. It is also sensitive to dynamic range. When the audio signal becomes weaker, the Dolby process increases its noise reduction processing. This is helpful because noise is more prevalent in the quiet parts of a recording. Where the audio signal is stronger, noise is less apparent and not as much Dolby processing is necessary. The noise reduction process follows the dynamics of the recording. The consumer version of the SR process is known as *Dolby S*.

All Dolby recordings are encoded in recording and should be decoded in playback. However, when making a copy of Dolby-encoded tapes, the boosted high frequencies will be part of the copy. Therefore, it is not necessary to decode and re-encode. The encoding will follow from copy to copy. It is only necessary to decode on final playback.

Out-of-Phase Audio

As with any signal based on sine waves, the waves of audio signals can be out of phase with each other. If the waves are 180° out of phase, or in other words, exactly opposite each other, cancellation will take place. When one wave is at its peak, the other would be at its low point. The result would be silence or near silence. Either side listened to alone would sound fine, as two signals are needed to create an out-of-phase situation. Signals less than 180° out of phase also cause a decrease in volume or amplitude but to a lesser degree.

Out-of-phase situations can be detected by a phase meter, a scope, or sometimes just by listening. Listening to one side then the other, and then both at once, will sometimes allow the detection of an out-of-phase situation. A drop in amplitude, when the two sides are listened to at once, will be an indication that the signals are out of phase.

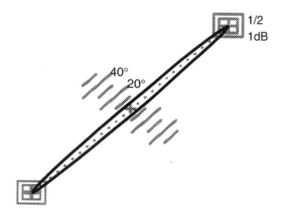

Figure 19.4 Out-of-Phase Audio

The out-of-phase error can be anywhere along the audio chain, from the original recording to the final playback. The audio may have been recorded out of phase. The speakers, through which the sound is coming, may have been wired incorrectly. Correcting this problem can sometimes be as simple as reversing two wires on one side of the signal path. By reversing one side only, the two sides would then be in phase with each other. This switch can be done anywhere along the audio path and the problem will be corrected.

If the audio is recorded out of phase, this can only be corrected by re-recording the audio in the correct phase relationship. It is possible to play back out-of-phase audio and, by phase reversing one side of the signal path, correct the phase for playback purposes.

Some digital scopes have a selection for checking stereo audio. If audio is present in the SDI stream, the signal will appear on the scope. If the audio is stereo and in phase, it will appear as a straight diagonal line. If audio is out of phase, the two lines appear separated by the amount they are out of phase. The signal in Figure 19.4 is slightly out of phase.

CHAPTER 20
Overview of Operations

Operational procedures for playing back and recording an analog video signal follow general principles regardless of the format, television standard, or the content of the signal. Digital video, because it is a serial stream of bits, is not subject to the errors, changes, and corrections required by analog signals and therefore the setup process is minimal.

VTR and VCR Components

All videotape machines have the same basic functions and parts. On open-reel machines, the parts are visible and accessible (Figure 20.1). On cassette-based machines, some of the parts are internal and are accessible only by opening the machine housing. The function controls may vary in their placement, but all machines have controls for similar parameters.

Every videotape machine has a *scanner,* also known as a drum. The scanner, which contains the video heads, is where the recording is created or reproduced. As the tape passes across the scanner, the video heads read or record information on the tape.

Following the scanner, there are *audio stacks* that record and play back the audio portion of the videotape. One audio stack plays the signal back in a playback mode. In a record mode, one stack erases any existing signal on the tape, while another records the incoming material. Some machines also have a monitor stack to allow monitoring playback of the audio while the recording is being made.

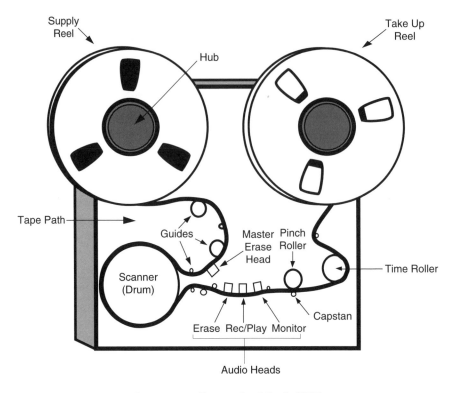

Figure 20.1 Parts of a 1-Inch VTR

On the takeup side of the scanner are the *capstan* and *pinch roller*. The capstan regulates the speed of the tape as it moves through the video-tape machine. The pinch roller holds the tape against the capstan.

Operational Controls

After loading a tape, the scanner needs to be started. On some machines, this happens automatically. Pressing the PLAY button will also set the scanner in motion (Figure 20.2, *A* and *B*). Pressing the STANDBY button will turn the scanner on in the event the scanner turns itself off. It can also be used to shut off the scanner manually.

The control for shuttling the video in forward or reverse may be either a knob or a set of buttons or both. Use of this control

Figure 20.2 Continued

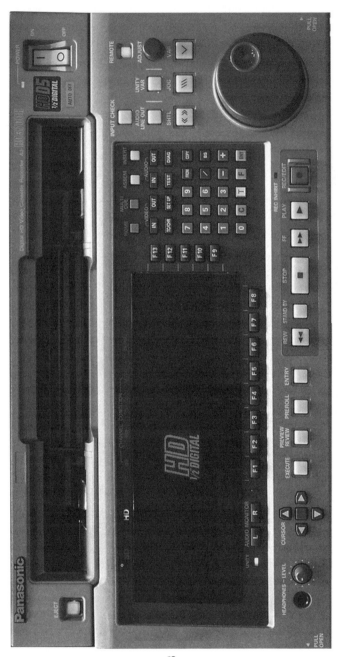

Figure 20.2 (continued) **A** and **B,** Betacam VCR and D5 VCR

will allow a variable movement of the tape at other than play speed. There may also be controls for FAST FORWARD and REWIND. The PLAY button will set the tape in motion at a normal forward speed for viewing. The STOP button will stop the motion of the tape without turning off the scanner. STOP can also be used at any time to stop a recording, an edit, or shuttle mode.

To make a recording it is necessary to press the PLAY and RECORD buttons simultaneously. Pressing both together will set the machine in forward motion at normal speed and begin recording immediately. To prevent an accidental recording, there is a switch marked RECORD LOCK-OUT. In the lock-out position, the machine will be prevented from going into record under any circumstances.

A REMOTE/LOCAL switch allows the machine to be controlled locally or from another location. In the LOCAL position, the machine can be operated at its own control panel. Quite often, putting a machine in REMOTE will not lock out all the LOCAL functions. This allows an operator some control over a machine that is being controlled from a remote location.

There is also a switch marked TAPE/EE. EE stands for electronics-to-electronics. In the EE mode, the incoming signal is passed through the machine without being affected by any of the machine settings. In the TAPE position, the video monitor displays the video that is on the tape no matter what mode the machine is in (e.g., stop, fast forward, rewind).

Audio is controlled by a series of knobs that adjust record and playback levels for all audio channels, and in some cases time code. There are meters above the knobs to show audio levels measured in VU. In some formats, time code level is not under the operator's control. In these cases, no meter will be available to monitor the level.

There is a meter for measuring VIDEO LEVEL, which is a separate reference than the waveform monitor. This meter may also be used to measure *RF*, or video signal strength, by selecting the button marked RF.

Either tape time or time code can be displayed on the video source. This display can be changed depending on the needs of the situation.

A jack is available for audio monitoring. This allows the use of a headset. When a headset is used, the audio may not be routed to the monitor speakers. A volume control is used to set the levels in the headset.

The main power switch for turning the machine ON and OFF is usually on the front panel. Occasionally, when a machine is having operating difficulties, powering it down and then turning it back on again will reset it and clear up the problem.

Analog Tape Playback

The video signal is in the physical form of magnetized metallic particles on the surface of the videotape. These particles are expanded and compressed as the tape is pulled through the machine. The actual amount that the videotape is altered as it plays is very minute. However, the critical timing intervals in the video signal are also very minute, millionths or billionths of a second. At that microscopic level, the stretching and relaxing of videotape produces very significant effects. A *time base corrector*, or *TBC*, corrects the irregularities created in the timing of the video signals.

The television image is a picture within a frame, with the active video portion being the picture itself, and the frame being the blanking area around the picture. Basically, the function of the time base corrector is to maintain the position of the picture within the frame and make the frame stable.

Time base correctors may also incorporate a *processing amplifier* or *proc amp*. A proc amp reprocesses the video signal to correct or alter signal levels. When adjusting the black level, video level, chroma level, and hue, it is actually the proc amp section of the TBC that is being controlled.

Analog Playback Procedures

When setting up for analog playback using color bars, the first step is to set the BLACK LEVEL or SETUP to 7.5 IRE units. The next step is to set the VIDEO LEVEL, or luminance, to 100 IRE units. Once the black and video levels are set, the next step is to adjust the CHROMA, or saturation. The reason why this particular order must be followed is that the measurement of each of the signals is dependent on the one prior.

Next, the CHROMA PHASE, or HUE, can be adjusted. Do not confuse this control with burst phase or system phase. The chroma phase or hue control will rotate the color vectors but leave the position of the color burst on its reference axis. Turn this control to align one of the vectors with its proper box.

To further adjust chroma, HI PASS or CHROMA and 2 FIELD or 2H can be selected on the waveform monitor. With this setting, the color bars can be viewed according to their saturation levels. The chip on the far right is blue. Yellow is on the left. The largest chip on the left is cyan and the largest chip on the right is red. The left chip in the center is green and the right chip in the center is magenta.

There are specific chroma levels at which the color chips should be set: Yellow and blue are 62 units each, 31 units above and 31 units below the base line marked on the scope. The next chips in on each side, cyan and red, are 88 units each, 44 units above and 44 units below the base line. The center set of chips is green and magenta, each being 82 units, 41 units above and 41 units below the base line.

The audio playback level controls are used to set the tone signal that is recorded with color bars on the tape. This level should be set to play back at zero VU on the audio meters.

Horizontal Blanking

Once playback levels have been set, blanking needs to be measured. This measurement is taken in the actual program content as opposed to color bars. The overall horizontal blanking period is the first measurement taken. This measurement should be taken with the waveform monitor set to FLAT, and 1 µs/DIV. The VERTICAL position control on the waveform monitor is used to position the sweep of the video signal so that the zero line is at -20 units. Active video at the base line will be at 20 units (Figure 20.3). The overall blanking width is measured from the front porch to the back porch. This measurement should be no smaller than 10.6 microseconds and no larger than 11.4 microseconds. The front porch should be 1.5 µs and the breezeway .5 µs.

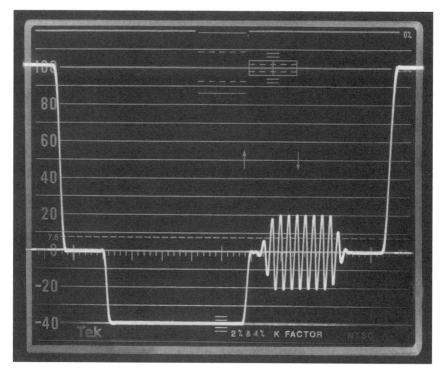

Figure 20.3 Horizontal Blanking

Once these measurements are taken, the vertical position of the sweep can be moved so that the zero line is positioned at +20 units on the graticule. This position places the mid-point of horizontal sync on the measuring line. In this position, the width of the horizontal sync pulse must be between 4.7 and 4.8 microseconds. The burst must have a minimum of 8 cycles and a maximum of 11 cycles at an amplitude of 40 IRE units, measured between −20 and +20 units.

Vertical Blanking

To measure the vertical blanking interval, the waveform monitor must be set for 2V or 2 FIELD magnified. There should be six pre-equalizing pulses and six vertical sync pulses. There will either be five or six post-equalizing pulses, depending on whether the even or odd field is being displayed. Active video should begin on line 20 or line 21 respectively (see Figure 4.4).

Video Recording

Before starting the recording process, it is important that the machine is set up for proper playback levels. A separate color bars reference tape can be used for this purpose. The audio tone should be set to play back at zero VU level. Once these levels are set, they will be the reference for the record levels.

The first step of making a recording is to record the incoming color bars signal. The next step is to check the incoming levels and compare them with the machine playback levels. This is done by switching between the EE signal and the playback signal off tape. At the record VTR, there is little control over what is being sent. If the incoming level is too low or too high, the signal must be corrected at the point of origination. Once the video levels are adjusted and set, the audio record levels can also be set.

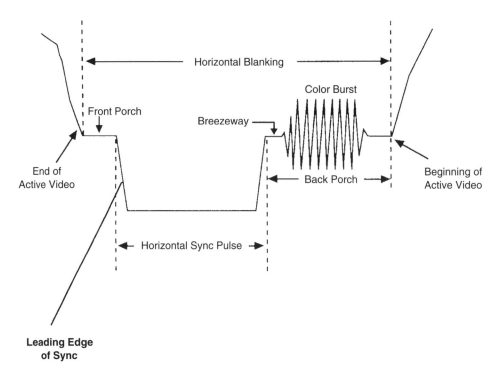

Figure 20.4 Leading Edge of Sync

Signal Timing

In order to create a coherent recording, the signal must follow certain guidelines and standards. Some of these standards dictate in very specific terms the timing of the signals contained in the video information. The synchronizing signal for the NTSC television system is the color subcarrier frequency.

To maintain the proper subcarrier phase relationship between sources, the NTSC system is designed to shift the picture horizontally so as to keep the subcarriers in phase. This shift is seen as a definite horizontal movement to the left or right. To eliminate this shift, a set of specifications was developed to define the subcarrier/horizontal, or SC/H relationship. This set of specifications is known as RS170A and refers to subcarrier/horizontal phasing.

RS170A states that the relationship between the color subcarrier and horizontal sync should be such that a zero crossing of the color subcarrier will occur at the 50% point of the leading edge of the horizontal sync pulse on Line 10 of each field. The leading edge of horizontal sync is the descending slope of the horizontal sync pulse (Figure 20.4). It follows the front porch in the horizontal blanking period. RS170A specifies that the point halfway down the slope of sync (−20 units) should coincide in time with a color subcarrier zero crossing point.

The timing differences involved in SC/H phasing are very small. Differences are measured in nanoseconds, or billionths of a second. In the color subcarrier signal, one cycle of subcarrier lasts for .279 microseconds or 279 nanoseconds. (This is rounded to 280 for mathematical convenience.) There are three zero crossing points in one cycle of subcarrier.

At the first zero crossing point, or anywhere up to the first quarter cycle (0°–90°), the system will align itself with the first zero crossing point (Figure 20.5), by shifting the picture horizontally to the left. If the subcarrier has passed the 90° point, and is therefore in the second quarter cycle (90°–180°), the system will align

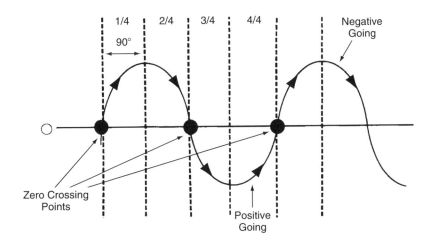

Figure 20.5 Subcarrier Cycle

itself with the second zero crossing point. The system will shift the image horizontally but in the opposite direction to the right.

As the cycle proceeds into the third quarter cycle (180°–270°), the second zero crossing point continues to be the reference. The second zero crossing point, then, is common to the second and third quarter cycles of the subcarrier wave. Finally, the fourth quarter cycle will reference to the third zero crossing point as the color subcarrier wave approaches the start of its next cycle. The system is never more than 90° or one quarter of a cycle off. One quarter of a cycle is equal to a duration of .07 microseconds or 70 nanoseconds.

Shifting the picture horizontally to the nearest zero crossing point may widen the blanking and may put the picture in an incorrect *color frame*. Color framing concerns the position of the subcarrier with respect to the lines and fields that make up the color picture. Since one cycle of subcarrier is 279 nanoseconds, or .279 microseconds, and one line of a television picture is $63\frac{1}{2}$ microseconds, there are $227\frac{1}{2}$ cycles of subcarrier per line.

This means that from line to line, the extra half cycle causes the phase of the subcarrier relative to the video to be opposite what it was in the previous line. In other words, if at the beginning of line 10 of a field, the color subcarrier is in its positive going direction (moving from lower left to upper right), then at the beginning of the next line of that field, it will be in a negative going direction (moving from upper left to lower right).

This relates to fields, in that if line 10 of the first field of a frame started with the color subcarrier going in a positive direction, then line 10 of the second field will have the color subcarrier going in a negative direction. The two fields that make up that one frame will have one field with a positive going subcarrier at its beginning and the second field will have a negative going subcarrier at its beginning.

At the beginning of the third color field (second frame, first field), the phase of the subcarrier will be negative going. In other words, if the first color field is positive going, and the second field is negative going, then the third color field will also be negative going. The next color field is the fourth in the series. It completes the second frame and it will be positive going. In this four-field system, the first field is positive, the second is negative, the third is negative, and the fourth is positive.

Continuing this process will show that the next field, or field five, begins positive going. The next field begins negative going, the field following that is negative going, and the field following that (field eight) is positive going, and so on.

When SC/H phase is to be checked, it is always measured on the tenth line, which is the first line that is common to both fields. In the odd field, the first full line of video begins on the tenth line. In the even field, however, the first half line of video begins on the ninth line. In any given color frame, there is one negative field and one positive field, negative and positive being defined as the direction of the subcarrier at the beginning of the tenth line.

Color framing, then, refers to the phase of the subcarrier. This four-field system must be adhered to in video editing in order for the subcarrier to be a continuous in-phase signal as one image is edited to another. If the four-field cycle is not adhered to, the subcarrier may become 180° out of phase when it crosses to the next color frame.

For example, an edit that placed two positive color frames next to each other would cause the phase of the subcarrier at the end of one color frame and the phase of the subcarrier at the beginning of the next color frame to go in the same direction. Instead of being a continuous signal, the color subcarrier at the second frame would be 180 degrees out of phase. This would cause an H (horizontal) shift at the edit point, as the system realigns itself. To help identify the proper sequence of fields in the color television signal, machines record a color frame pulse as part of the control track.

In PAL systems, the color framing process is the same except that there is a four-frame, eight-field requirement. As there are two burst reference signals to account for, the system requires more frames and fields to return to the proper color frame reference. In

SECAM systems, editing does not use a color reference. The video signal is edited in non-composite form. As there is no fixed burst reference, it is not possible to make composite color edits. The sync signals for video and chroma are added after the project is complete.

Insert and Assemble Editing

There are two ways to record in the edit mode, Insert and Assemble. In the *Insert* mode, the existing control track remains unchanged while the new video or audio is recorded or inserted over existing audio or video tracks. In the *Assemble* mode, new control track is recorded along with video and all-audio tracks.

In the Insert edit mode, there must be clean, continuous control track for the full length of the edit. Often tapes are pre-recorded with a video signal such as black or color bars for the length of the tape in order to prepare the tape for insert editing. In the Assemble edit mode, this is not necessary as new control track is recorded along with the new audio and video information during each edit.

When making an insert edit into existing material, it is necessary to set the record machine's audio and video record levels to match those of the existing material. Set the record machine's playback levels by using the bars at the head of the record tape.

In the Assemble mode, the OUT point of an edit will always be "dirty," meaning that instead of a clean cut at the end of the edit, there will be a ragged falling off of video. An assemble edit made into existing material may ruin the material that follows it and leave an irreparable hole in the control track. The beginning of an assemble edit, however, is clean.

Digital Playback and Recording

Because of the consistency of digital data and the ability to incorporate error correction, the process of recording and playing back digital information is greatly simplified. While it is still necessary to verify the accuracy of the incoming or transmitted signal, digital signals left in unity, or the preset machine levels, generally will not need to be adjusted.

CHAPTER 21

Test Signals, Displays, and Media Problems

Unlike program material, test signals are designed to assist in achieving precisely defined measurements in the video signal. They are used to determine whether a piece of equipment or system is working properly, to measure noise levels in the signal, chroma errors, errors that occur in the converging of the chroma and luminance signals, and to measure signal levels to ensure they meet proper standards. There is a multitude of test signals, each one designed to measure a specific aspect of the television signal.

Both the digital and analog domains make use of some of the same test signals. However, because analog and digital signals are prone to different types of errors, the way test signals are examined and analyzed differs between the two domains. In the digital domain, the displays used on the waveform and vectorscope examine properties of a digital test signal that do no exist in analog.

Color Bars

The primary test signal in video is *color bars*. Color bars come in several different presentations, including full field bars, EIA split field bars, SMPTE, and PLUGE bars. These were developed over time to address different aspects of the video setup process.

The EIA split field bars contain a 100% white chip, a 75% white chip, and the three primary and three secondary colors. The analog black setup chip is 7.5 IRE units. In digital, the black setup chip is zero (Figure 21.1). In analog, the I and Q chips are used to determine if the color is being created correctly by the encoder and to set the phase on a vectorscope. If the I, Q, and burst signals are not in their exact relationship to each other in the analog signal, then the color information that results will be incorrect.

Color bars can be generated from several different sources: from a camera encoder, from a *color bar generator,* or from a sync generator with a color bar pattern output. When the color bar signal is coming from a camera encoder, it represents the way the camera has been set up. The encoder is creating the color bars in the same way it will process the video when the camera is switched over to a picture mode. The bars coming out of the encoder are created by the same electronics that will create the television picture.

Stairstep

Theoretically, analog television systems should handle chroma equally through all luminance levels. High luminance colors and

Figure 21.1 PLUGE Bar Display

low luminance colors should be carried through the system without distortion of levels. In practice, chrominance signals are not always reproduced accurately. Errors in chroma reproduction are possible between the lowest luminance signals and the highest luminance signals.

The stairstep test signal was created to determine the accuracy of reproduced chroma signals during changes in luminance. The stairstep signal displays a consistent chroma level through changing luminance levels. Color subcarrier is used as the chrominance signal, as it is the main carrier of the color information in the system and common to all colors.

The stairstep signal is a set of luminance chips from 7.5 to 100 IRE units in 5, 10, or 20-unit steps. There is no true color in the signal. There is only color subcarrier running through a series of luminance chips (Figure 21.2)

Multiburst

Multiburst is a test signal that was created to identify how a system handles different frequencies at the same luminance level. In some ways, it is the other side of the coin of the stairstep signal. Stairstep measures a fixed chroma level over varying luminance levels, whereas multiburst measures varying frequencies over a fixed luminance level.

Analog video is recorded using a frequency modulated process. The variations in frequency imposed on the carrier represent the changes in levels of the video. In theory, a television system should reproduce all frequencies equally without altering the original values. In reality, due to the imprecise nature of analog recording, various frequencies are often altered from their true values during the record process. Therefore, when playing back such a recording, light and dark areas may appear brighter or darker than they actually are.

Multiburst is a series of "bursts" or pieces of various frequencies. Multiburst is a 50% luminance level and the frequencies

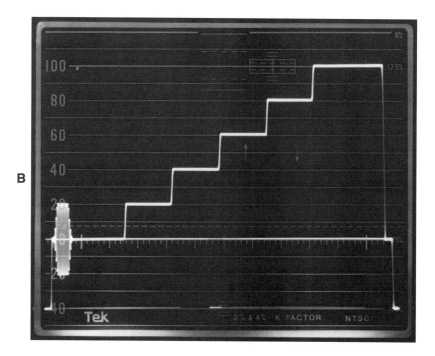

Figure 21.2 A, Stairstep Image and **B,** Stairstep on Scope

included are usually ½ megahertz, 1 megahertz, 2 megahertz, 3 megahertz, 3.6 megahertz, and 4.2 megahertz. This range covers the frequency spectrum of the television system, including the approximate frequency of the color subcarrier (Figure 21.3).

In the multiburst signal, there is no chroma information, as it is a luminance test pattern. The multiburst is tied in with color in the sense that most of the color information is high frequency and the luminance information is low frequency. An increase or decrease in either one would cause some colors to appear oversaturated or undersaturated.

As multiburst is also used to measure and compare the abilities of a system's machines, monitors, and tapes to reproduce the fine detail in an image, it is useful in digital video as well as analog. A lack of ability to handle high frequency signals results in a blurring of fine edges in an image.

Cross Hatch

It is possible for the top or bottom of a monitor's image to compress or slant inward. This is called *keystoning*. The term keystone refers to the "key" stone in an arch. The key stone is wider at the top than at the bottom. Therefore, a television picture that is wider at the top than at the bottom, or vice versa, is said to be keystoned. The image may also curve inward on the sides. This is called *pin cushioning*, named after the shape of early pin cushions used in sewing. These problems may occur due to misadjustments in the scanning sweep within the monitor's electronics. The test signal used to deter-mine if these problems exist in a monitor is *cross hatch*, also called *linearity*.

Cross hatch is a series of horizontal and vertical white lines on a black field that form a series of square boxes on the monitor. In some displays, a white dot is put in the center of each box (Figure 21.4). The horizontal and vertical lines in the cross hatch signal will reflect distortions that create keystoning or pin cushioning effects.

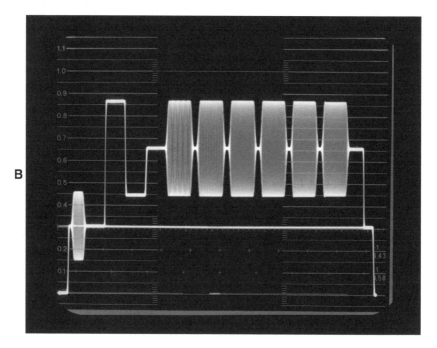

Figure 21.3 A, Multiburst Image and **B,** Multiburst on Scope

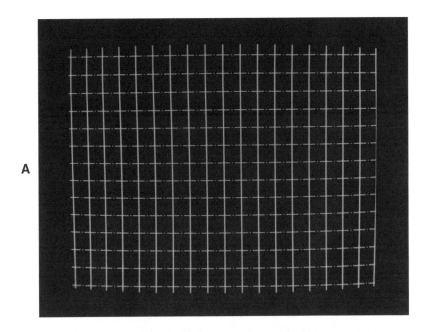

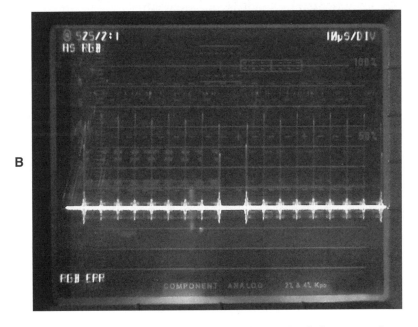

Figure 21.4 A, Cross Hatch Image and **B,** Cross Hatch Image on Scope

Cross hatch is also used to check for alignment or registration of the color beams in a monitor. If the beams in the monitor are not properly aligned, there will be color fringes on the cross hatch lines. On a properly aligned monitor, the squares on the monitor should all appear to be of equal size, perfectly square with each other, all the way out to the corners and edges of the screen. The entire display should have perfect white lines without any color fringing.

Digital Displays

There are several test displays that are unique to digital video. One of these is the *Diamond* display. The function of the Diamond display is to define the color space or *gamut* of the image. The way the gamut is identified is by simple vectors that represent colors. Together, these vectors form two diamond shapes (Figure 21.5). Any signal that is outside of these diamonds, or this color gamut, is outside the color space limits and may not be reproducible by a color monitor. This display is used to ensure that the color portion of the signal is not oversaturated. If the signal is oversaturated, the portions of the image outside the diamond area may be clipped or limited to colors within the gamut.

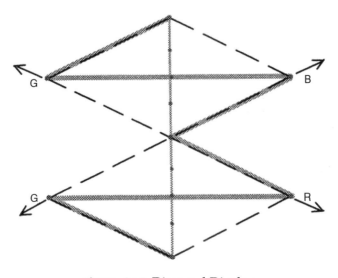

Figure 21.5 Diamond Display

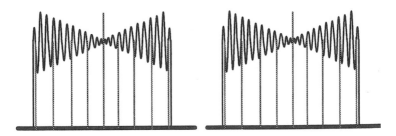

Figure 21.6 Bowtie Display

Another display used to view a digital signal is the *Bowtie* display, which has two purposes. The first is to ensure that the luminance signal and the color difference signals are timed to occur simultaneously. It is important that these signals converge at the same time so that a complete and correct image will be created. The second purpose of the Bowtie display is to ensure that the gain or amplitude of these signals, luminance, and color difference, match as well. The Bowtie shows the composite of the color and luminance signals together as one display. This display is named after the bowtie shape of the signal (Figure 21.6).

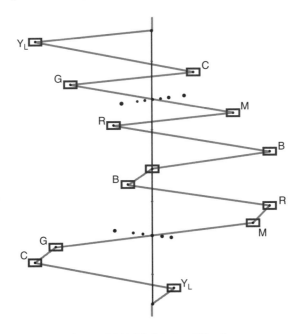

Figure 21.7 Lightning Display

A third digital display is the *Lightning* display, which takes the form of a lightning bolt (Figure 21.7). The Lightning display compares the color difference signals (P_BP_R) with the luminance signal (Y). This display, as opposed to the Bowtie, shows the individual colors over the range of luminance levels rather than a composite of all the signals. The Lightning display is used when adjusting luminance levels. It is important that the relationship between the quantity of color (saturation) and the luminance level (video) remains constant or that any increase or decrease in luminance is accompanied by a corresponding increase or decrease in color saturation. In this way, the lightning display shows any error caused by changes within luminance or chrominance that do not track with each other.

Analog Tape Problems

Videotape as a recording medium has a number of problems associated with it. Some of them are due to improper handling and some are due to normal tape wear. If handled properly, a videotape is good for dozens of passes through a VTR. These problems are not as extensive in cassette tape formats.

One of the problems of analog videotape recording is *dropouts*. Dropouts are missing microscopic bits of oxide on the tape. They appear on a monitor as missing lines or portions of lines of video information. Most machines have what are called *dropout compensators,* or *DOCs*. DOCs fill in the missing video by using the previous line of good video. When the dropouts become excessive, or there are large quantities of missing oxide, the result is noticeable even when using the dropout compensator.

Creases and *wrinkles* come from poor handling of a videotape or from a machine malfunction. Once a tape is creased or wrinkled, it may not be able to be run through the machine without the risk of damage to the machine and the video heads.

All videotape *stretches* initially from normal starting, stopping, and shuttling procedures, but that is compensated for in the design of the machine itself. The type of stretching that becomes a problem comes from using the same piece of tape over and over in the same area.

Digital Tape Problems

Tape stretching is not a problem in digital formats because the information on tape is digital data, and not an analog signal. Also, digital tape formats have a built-in ability to detect an error, and then either conceal it or correct it on playback. Errors in digital magnetic media take the form of missing data bits. This missing information is detected during playback. Rather than simply repeat the prior information as with an analog dropout compensator, the microprocessor examines the prior data and the following data and calculates what the missing information might be. The machine then creates the missing data bits and includes that data at the output of the machine.

In this manner, any distortion of data due to creases, wrinkles, dropouts, and so on, can be detected and concealed, or in some cases, corrected. Digital machines have the capability of reporting on the monitor whether missing information has been detected and whether the error has been concealed or corrected.

Optical Media Problems

In the case of optical media, there is no possibility of dropouts or lost data. However, optical media, because it is plastic based, is prone to two forms of damage: scratches and warping. Scratches create a defraction problem with the laser beam used to read the data. The scratch causes the beam to become scattered or incoherent. Scratches can be repaired by polishing the surface of the CD or DVD or coating the surface with a material that prevents the dispersion of the laser beam.

Warping, caused by heat or improper storage, is not a correctable problem. If the disk is warped, the distance that the laser travels is altered and the data cannot be reproduced correctly. A disk that is warped cannot be straightened or corrected.

Hard Drive Failures

Hard drives, because they are mechanical, are subject to mechanical failures. These would include bearing problems, overheating, and contact between the read/write head and the surface of the disk. Hard drives are mounted on bearings that reduce friction as the disk spins. If the bearings fail, the disk will seize and stop turning. Bearings can fail due to a loss of lubrication or from overheating.

The read/write head transfers data to the surface of the disk without actually making contact. If it does make contact with the disk surface, it causes damage and can destroy the data. If the disk has not been severely damaged, it can be removed from the drive, placed in a new drive, and the data retrieved.

Hard drive failures can be overcome through a system of redundant information spread over several disks. Through a RAID system, a Redundant Array of Independent Disks, the data is duplicated over several drives. A failure of one drive does not result in the loss of data. Also, replacement of a defective drive can occur without any interruption.

In Summary

The theory and operations of video can be a challenging subject to pursue. At the present time and for the foreseeable future, the industry is going through a period of great change as are most elements of the communications field. Continuing your understanding of the area will require ongoing study and education. While this book has laid the foundation for a basic knowledge of how video works, it will continue to be updated to reflect the major changes within the video industry.

Glossary

4:2:0 A digital compression scheme. For every four samples of luminance taken, two are taken for each color difference signal, but only on every other scan line. (See 4:2:2.)

4:2:2 A digital compression scheme. For every four samples of luminance taken, two are taken for each of the color difference signals.

4:4:4 A digital compression scheme. For every four samples of luminance taken, four are taken for each of the color difference signals.

Active Video The portion of the video signal that contains program material.

Additive Color System The color system in which adding all colors together produces white. It is an active color system in that the object being viewed is generating the visible light as opposed to reflecting another light source. The television system is an additive color process.

Address Track The time code channel created for the $\frac{3}{4}$-inch cassette format. The address track is imbedded in the video track, thus leaving the two exisiting audio channels available for program material.

AFM (Audio Frequency Modulation) A method, developed by Sony, for recording audio in the video track of a BetaSP recording. The AFM channels yield a higher quality audio signal than the standard longitudinal audio tracks. Unlike the longitudinal audio tracks, these tracks can only be recorded along with video.

Amplitude Modulation (AM)   A change or modulation in the height or amplitude imposed on a carrier signal. The changes in amplitude are analogous to voltage variations in the signal. In television, it is the method used for transmission of video information.

Analog   In television, a signal that uses a continuously varying voltage to represent the outputs from equipment for the purpose of recording, playing back, or transmitting.

Aperture   The dot of electron illumination that occurs where the beam intersects the face of the target. The dot or beam aperture is the smallest size that an element of picture information can be.

Aspect Ratio   The mathematical relationship between the width and the height of an image. The standard NTSC, PAL, and SECAM analog aspect ratio for television is four units wide by three units high, shown as 4×3. The aspect ratio for High Definition television is 16×9.

ATSC   The Advanced Television Systems Committee. The next generation of the NTSC, it is the group responsible for the creation of digital SDTV and HDTV in the United States.

Assemble Edit   A type of edit where control track is laid down along with the video and audio.

Auto Edit Mode   The capability of a VTR to go in and out of an edit automatically at pre-selected points.

B Frames   The Bi-directional frames indicated in an MPEG compression system. The data they contain are extracted from previous and/or following frames and thus are referred to as bi-directional. These frames cannot stand alone as they contain only portions of the video data from each frame.

Back Porch   The period of time during horizontal blanking that follows the horizontal sync pulse and continues to the beginning of active video.

Bias   The recording of a very high frequency audio signal at a low energy level on a tape. The signal overcomes the tape's resistance to recording the incoming signals.

Binary   A system of numbers consisting of zeros and ones only. The language in which computers store and manipulate information.

Bit   In digital or computer information, a zero or a one.

Bit Rate   The number of bits per second moving through a digital system, expressed as bps.

Black Burst   A composite signal that combines the color subcarrier, horizontal sync, vertical sync, blanking, and a black video signal. It is also known as Color Black.

Black Level   The measurement of the black portion of the video signal. In an analog television system, this should not go below 7.5 IRE units. In a digital video system, black may be zero units.

Bowtie   On a digital waveform monitor, a display used to check and confirm the coincidence of the luminance and chrominance signals.

Breezeway   The part of the horizontal blanking period that goes from the end of the horizontal sync pulse to the beginning of the color burst cycle.

Burst   Eight to eleven cycles of pure subcarrier that appear on the back porch during horizontal blanking. The burst is used as a reference to synchronize color circuits in a receiver with the transmitted color signals. It is not modulated and does not have any of the other chroma information in it, such as hue and saturation.

Calibrate   The process of standardizing a reference tool, such as a vectorscope or waveform monitor, so that any signal information that is displayed is measured accurately.

Captioning/Closed Captioning   Developed to aid the hearing impaired, the process of encoding and decoding typed text so that it may be displayed on a receiver or monitor. In the NTSC closed captioning system, the data is incorporated on line 21.

Charge Coupled Device (CCD)   A solid state device or chip consisting of multiple sites operating as capacitors that convert light energy to electrical charges.

Chrominance   Pure color information without light or luminance references.

Color Bars   A test signal that provides the necessary elements for visual setup of video equipment. The basic display includes a white or video-level reference, black-level reference, chroma levels, and hue information. Additional elements also may be included.

Color Black/Black Burst   A composite signal that combines the color subcarrier, horizontal sync, vertical sync, blanking, and a black video signal.

Color Difference Signal   The calculation of the quantity of chroma information in the signal minus the luminance (Y) information (i.e., R-Y, B-Y, and G-Y).

Color Encoding   Translating the color video information from its original state to a condensed form for recording and transmitting.

Color Frame Pulse   A pulse recorded on videotape that identifies the color frame cycle.

Color Framing   The phase or direction of the subcarrier signal with respect to the lines and fields that make up the color picture. In the NTSC system, the color frame is determined by the phase of the color subcarrier at the beginning of line 10 of the first field of each frame. In the NTSC system, there are four fields to the color frame cycle. In the PAL system there are eight fields to the color frame cycle.

Color Gamut   The allowable range, minimum and maximum, of the color difference signals. Within this range, colors will be reproduced accurately on a picture monitor or receiver. Outside this range, certain colors may be either distorted or not reproduced at all.

Color Subcarrier   An additional carrier for the color information, which is transmitted and recorded within the main carrier of the video signal.

Component   Individual element that represents a part of the composite signal. In component television, these elements include Y (luminance), R-Y, and B-Y (the color difference signals), or R, G, and B (the individual color signals).

Composite   A complete video signal that includes all sync signals, blanking signals, and active video. Active video contains luminance and chrominance information encoded into one signal. Composite sync includes horizontal and vertical sync and vertical pre- and post-equalizing pulses.

Compression   The process of reducing data in a digital signal by eliminating redundant information.

Control Track   A recorded signal on videotape that allows the VTR scanner or head to align itself with the beginning of each video track. One control track pulse occurs for each revolution of the scanner.

Cross Hatch   A test signal that displays horizontal and vertical lines that can be used to determine whether a video monitor is distorting the video image. Also called linearity, such distortion might include pin cushioning, keystoning, and color fringing caused by misalignment of the color guns.

Cross Pulse A monitor display that shows both the horizontal and vertical blanking periods. Also known as Pulse Cross.

Cue Track An audio track in digital video recording used for locating sections or scenes when the tape is in a shuttle or jog mode.

Decibel A logarithmic relationship between two power values. In audio it is used to measure the intensity of sound. Notated as dB, there are several variations of decibel measurements.

Decoding The process of reconstituting encoded recorded or transmitted information back to its original state. Some of the original information may be lost in the initial encoding process and will be unrecoverable during decoding.

Deflection Coils In a video camera or receiver, the device that moves the beam across the face of the target or picture tube. Horizontal deflection coils cause the electron beam to scan from side to side for individual lines. Vertical deflection coils cause movement of the beam up or down to the next line and cause retrace to occur at the end of each field.

Demodulate To take a modulated signal that is imposed on a carrier and recreate the information it represents in its original form.

Diamond Display A simplified display on a vector scope for the RGB color component signals that indicates the valid limits for the color gamut.

Differential Gain The measurement of the difference in saturation levels that can occur between low luminance colors (e.g., blue) and high luminance colors (e.g., yellow).

Differential Phase The errors in hue that can occur between low luminance colors (e.g., blue) and high luminance colors (e.g., yellow).

Digital A system that uses binary bits or digits to represent sine wave or analog information.

Dolby Originally, a technique for audio noise reduction developed by Ray Dolby and Dolby Laboratories, it is also a standardized system for 5.1 channel surround sound called Dolby Digital AC-3.

Down Converting Converting a video signal from a scanning standard with a high pixel count to one with a lower pixel count.

Downlink A facility for receiving signals from a satellite.

Drive Pulse The signals used in an analog video system that cause interlace scanning to occur. Drive pulses are used for both horizontal and vertical scanning of the electron beam.

Drop Frame A type of time code in which the time code generator drops, or actually skips, two numbers, 00 and 01, every minute except the 10th minute Drop frame time code is clock accurate.

Dropouts Missing microscopic bits of oxide on a videotape that appear on a monitor as missing lines of video information.

Electron Beam A stream of electrons used to convert light energy to an electrical signal as in a camera pickup tube, or to convert electrical energy to light as in a monitor or cathode ray tube.

Electron Gun That part of the pickup tube or receiver that produces the electron beam.

Encoding In general, the process of compressing data for storage or transmission purposes.

Equalization A boosting or attenuating of certain frequencies when a signal is recorded or played back so as to more accurately represent or purposely alter the original signals.

Equalizing Pulses Pulses that assure continued synchronization of the video signals during vertical retrace as well as proper interlace of the odd and even fields of video.

External Sync   A synchronizing reference that is coming from an external source.

FCC   The Federal Communications Commission. The commission that regulates the practices and procedures of the communications industries in the United States.

Field   One half of a scanned image. A field can be referred to as an odd field or an even field. In the NTSC system, each field is made up of 262-1/2 lines. There are 2 fields per frame, and 60 fields per second. In the PAL and SECAM standards, there are 312-1/2 lines per field, 2 fields per frame, and 50 fields per second.

Footprint   The area of the earth that a satellite signal covers.

Frame   The combination of the odd and even fields of a video signal. In each frame of NTSC video, there are 525 lines of information, and there are 30 frames in a second. In the PAL and SECAM standards there are 25 frames per second, each frame containing 625 lines.

Frequency Modulation (FM)   A change in the frequency of the signal imposed on a carrier. Frequency changes reflect voltage variations from the output of the originating source. In television, it is the method used for recording analog video information on tape and for the transmission of audio signals.

Front Porch   That period of time during horizontal blanking that starts at the end of active video and continues to the leading edge of the horizontal sync pulse.

Gop   The defined Group of Pictures used in the MPEG compression process. The GOP will contain an I frame and may contain B frames and P frames. The group may consist of as few as 1 frame or as many as 30 or more.

Graticule   A lined screen in front of a CRT on a waveform or vectorscope, which is used to measure and define the specifications of a signal.

Geosynchronous   When satellites are placed in orbit, they are set in motion to move at the same speed as the rotation of the earth, making them stationary above the earth. The geosynchronous orbit is set at 22,300 miles above the earth.

Harmonics   The multiplication of frequencies achieved by adding the initial frequency or fundamental to itself in an arithmetic progression.

HDTV   High Definition Television. The high resolution standard for video. HDTV includes a high pixel count, increased line count, and a wider aspect ratio.

Hertz   Anything measured in "cycles per second" or the number of changes that occur within one second.

Head   Individual parts of a tape machine that either erase, record, or play back signals on a tape.

Horizontal Blanking   The period of time in which the electron beam is turned off while it is repositioned to start scanning the next line.

Horizontal Drive Pulses   Pulses that cause the electron beam to scan horizontally across the face of the target in a tube camera.

Horizontal Resolution   The amount of detail that can be achieved horizontally across an image. This is generally measured as the number of vertical lines that can be accurately recreated horizontally across the screen. In film it is measured in the number of lines per millimeter. In video this is measured by the frequency of the signal that can still be seen as individual black and white lines.

Horizontal Synchronizing Pulses   That part of the video signal that ensures that all of the equipment used in the creation, transmission, and reception of the video signal is synchronized on a line-by-line basis.

Hue   A specific color or pigment. In television, one of the elements that makes up the composite color signal. A hue is represented by a vector on the vectorscope.

I And Q Vectors   The In-phase and Quadrature vectors along which color video information is encoded in the NTSC video standard.

I Frame-   In the MPEG compression process, the Intraframe. The frame that contains all the image data and needs no reference to the preceding or following frames. Used as the reference frame for the creation of the B and P frames.

Image Resolution   The amount of detail contained in a video image based on the number of lines in the image and the number of pixels per line.

Infrared   Frequencies above 100 gigahertz and below 432 trillion hertz. Infrared is above the broadcast spectrum and below the visible spectrum. Infrared can be felt as heat.

Insert Edit   A type of edit where new video or audio is recorded onto existing material. The existing control track remains unchanged.

Interlace Scanning   The process of combining two fields of video information. One field has the odd lines of the scanned image and the other field has the even lines. The two fields are interlaced together to form one complete image or frame of video.

Internal Sync   A sync reference that is generated within a piece of equipment.

IRE   Institute of Radio Engineers. A measurement of units of video information on the waveform monitor graticule. One volt of video is divided into 140 IRE units.

JPEG   Joint Photographic Experts Group. A process of lossy image compression used for still images.

Keystoning   When the top or bottom of a television image is compressed or less than full width. The name is derived from the shape of the stone placed at the top of an arch.

Leading Edge of Sync   The descending slope of the horizontal sync pulse that follows the front porch.

Lightning Display   A display on a waveform monitor that plots the two color difference signals against the luminance signal. Used to measure the color accuracy over the luminance gain to detect any timing delay between the color signals and the luminance signal.

Line Frequency   In the NTSC monochrome system, 15,750 lines per second, a multiple of 525 lines per frame at 30 frames per second. In the NTSC color system, approximately 15, 734 lines per second, yielding 29.97 frames per second.

Linearity   See Cross Hatch.

Longitudinal Time Code   Time code recorded and reproduced as an audio signal.

Lossless Compression   In lossless compression, the restored image is an exact duplicate of the original with no loss of data.

Lossy Compression   In lossy compression, the restored image is an approximation, not an exact duplicate, of the original.

Low Pass   A filter that passes luminance data and filters out the higher frequency color information.

Luminance   The amount of white light in an image.

Manual Edit Mode   The mode in which edits can be made "on the fly" without preset entry or exit points.

Modulated Carrier   A specific frequency upon which changes have been made to carry or transmit information. There are two ways to modulate or change a carrier, amplitude modulation (AM) and frequency modulation (FM).

MPEG   Moving Picture Experts Group. A lossy compression process used to reduce the data requirements for moving images. There are several variations, from MPEG-1 to MPEG-21.

MP3   MPEG Audio Layer 3. An audio compression standard generally used to reduce the storage requirements for music.

Multiburst   A test signal used to measure the capability of a video system or monitor to reproduce a range of frequencies. The range of frequencies tested is generally from .5 Mhz through 4.5 Mhz.

Non-Drop Frame   A type of time code used to label every video frame in numerically consecutive order. It is not altered to reflect the slower frame rate of color television, i.e., it is not clock accurate.

NTSC   National Television System Committee. A method for creating composite analog monochrome television. Also, a method used to create color television based on color difference components modulated on one color subcarrier.

Octave   In television and video, a doubling of a frequency.

Oscilloscopes   A type of measuring tool that uses a CRT to display and measure signal strength, frequency, and amplitude.

One Volt "Peak-to-Peak"   The strength of a video signal measured from −40 IRE units to 100 IRE units in analog. In digital video, one volt is measured in millivolts, from −300 to 700 millivolts.

PAL   Phase Alternate Line. A method for creating composite analog color video. The PAL system makes use of two color subcarriers simultaneously that are phase inverted from each other on alternate scan lines.

Parade   A display on a waveform monitor that simultaneously displays the luminance signal and the two color difference signals in sequential order.

Pedestal   The black level in the video signal. Also called setup.

Persistence of Vision   The period of time that the retina, or light-sensitive part of the eye, retains an image. The phenomenon that allows individual images to be perceived as continuous motion.

P Frames   In the MPEG compression process, the predictive frames. P frames contain only data that is different from the I Frame. They are not complete images and cannot stand alone.

Packets   In the data stream, after the data has been segmented to prepare for transmission, it is inserted in a packet. Packets are then contained in frames.

Pickup Tube   The tube inside a camera that converts light into an electrical signal.

Pin Cushioning   When the picture curves in along the sides. Named after the old-style pin cushions used for holding pins for sewing.

Pixels   Picture elements. The individual elements that make up a digital image.

Pluge   Picture Line Up and Generating Equipment. An SMPTE color bar display that may be used to correctly calibrate a picture monitor.

Post-Equalizing Pulses   Six pulses that occur after vertical sync at twice the line frequency. They assure continued synchronization during vertical retrace as well as proper interlace of the odd and even fields of video.

Pre-Equalizing Pulses   Six pulses that occur before vertical sync at twice the line frequency. They assure continued synchronization during vertical retrace as well as proper interlace of the odd and even fields of video.

Preroll   The amount of time VTRs need to stabilize and synchronize before making an edit.

Primary Color   In a defined color system, a color that cannot be created through a combination of any of the other primary colors.

Preview   A look at how an edit would be if it were recorded, without actually recording the video.

Progressive Scan   The recording and recreation of an image as a complete line-by-line frame from a single point in time.

PsF   Progressive Segmented Frame. A progressively scanned image that has been divided into two fields, each containing alternate lines from the frame. Unlike a true interlaced frame, both fields are from the same point in time.

Pulse Cross   See Cross Pulse.

Raid   A Redundant Array of Independent Disks. The recording of data redundantly over more than one hard drive disk to prevent catastrophic loss. There are several varieties of RAIDs providing various levels of protection.

Retrace   During the scanning process, the return path of the electron beam.

RF   Radio Frequency. That portion of the spectrum that lies between 3Khz and 300Ghz.

Sampling Rate   The rate at which analog data is read and the result is converted to digital information.

SAP   Separate Audio Program. In televsion recordings and transmission, a separate audio channel reserved for foreign languages.

Saturation   The ratio of luminance to chrominance information (e.g., the difference between red and pink).

Sawtooth Waveform Generator   A circuit in a video camera that is used to trigger the horizontal and vertical deflection of the electron beam. The name "sawtooth" refers to the shape of the signal the generator creates, which looks like the serrations on the edge of a wood saw.

SC/H Phasing   The relationship between the phase of the color subcarrier and the horizontal sync pulse. SC/H stands for Subcarrier/Horizontal.

Scanner   That portion of a VTR that houses the video heads. Also called the drum.

SDI   Serial Digital Interface. The SMPTE standard for SDI has a data rate of between 143 Mb/s or megabits per second and 360 Mb/s.

SDTV   Standard Definition Television. The name given to the original NTSC, PAL, and SECAM television standards.

Secam   Sequential Colour Avec Memoire. A television standard using 625 scan lines per frame at 25 frames per second, developed by the French and used in several Eastern European countries. In the SECAM standard, there is no fixed color reference. All editing and image switching must be done as non-composite video with the synchronizing done after the fact.

Secondary Colors   Those colors that are created by combining any two of the primary colors. In the NTSC system, the secondary colors are yellow, cyan, and magenta.

Setup   The black level in the video signal. Also called pedestal.

Signal-to-Noise Ratio   The relationship between the strength of the desired signal and the strength of the background noise or undesired information, expressed as a ratio S/N.

SMPTE   The Society of Motion Picture and Television Engineers. The organization that sets the technical standards for television and motion pictures in the United States.

Stereo   An audio system consisting of discrete left and right channels.

Stair Step   A type of test signal that is used to check Differential Gain.

Subtractive Color System   The physical principle by which the eye perceives color in most objects. In the subtractive system, an object absorbs all colors except that which the object is perceived to be. That color is reflected and stimulates the retina of the eye. In the subtractive color process, the addition of all colors will yield black, as all colors will be absorbed and none reflected. (See also ADDITIVE COLOR SYSTEM.)

Surround Sound   An audio system consisting of front, side, and rear speakers that creates a realistic audio environment in which the sound surrounds the listener.

Synchronizing Generator   The piece of equipment that produces the synchronizing signals, such as horizontal and vertical blanking, horizontal and vertical sync, and color burst, that keeps all video equipment in time with each other.

Target   The face of the pickup tube that is scanned by the electron beam.

Teletext   Information that is sent along with the video signal that can be viewed separately from program material. Examples include a list of programs on a cable station or the local weather and news.

Test Signals   Signals such as color bars, stair step, multiburst, and cross hatch that are used in the setting up and checking of television equipment.

Time Base Corrector   A piece of equipment that corrects errors in the timing during the playback of recorded video signals. These errors occur due to the mechanical nature of video equipment.

Time Code   A labeling system that is used to identify each frame of recorded video. There are several systems of time code in use worldwide.

Trace   The process of scanning a line of video information. This scanning or tracing process occurs a line at a time.

Transcoding   Converting a video signal with one color encoding method into a signal with a different encoding method. Also in digital, various methods for recoding a compressed bit stream or decompressing and recompressing the data.

Transponders   A channel of communication on a satellite.

Upconverting   Converting a video signal from one scanning standard to another with a higher pixel count.

Uplink   A facility for the transmission of signals to a satellite.

Vector   A mathematical representation of a force in a particular direction. In television, it is used to measure color information where the angle represents the hue and the length represents the saturation.

Vectorscope   A type of oscilloscope that is used to display the saturation and the hue of the video signal.

Vertical Blanking   The period of time in which the electron beam is turned off while it moves from the bottom of the image to the top of the image to begin tracing or scanning the next field of video.

Vertical Drive Pulse   An electronic pulse that moves the electron beam down the face of the pickup tube one line at a time during field scanning. It also moves the beam back to the top of the picture during vertical blanking.

Vertical Interval   That portion of the video signal that includes the vertical blanking, the vertical sync pulses, and the pre- and post-equalizing pulses. Also, the area where other information that is carried with the television signal, such as captioning, teletext, and satellite instructions, is inserted.

Vertical Interval Reference Signal (VIRS)   The VIRS provides a constant color reference for the monitor or receiver. Without the VIRS, the color balance of the image could change.

Vertical Interval Test Signals (VITS)   One of several different one-line test signals that are inserted into one of the unused video lines in the vertical interval providing a constant reference with respect to the active video contained within the frame.

Vertical Interval Time Code   A visual encoding of time code inserted into the vertical interval. As the data is visual, the information may be read when the image is not moving.

Vertical Resolution   The detail in an image dictated by the number of horizontal scan lines the image contains.

Video Level   A measurement of the luminance level of the video image. In NTSC, the analog video level should not exceed 100 IRE units nor go below 7-1/2 IRE units. In digital images, black may be 0 millivolts and peak video may be 700 millivolts.

VU   Volume Units. Properly noted as dBVU, it is a measurement of the strength of an audio signal. Traditionally, 0 VU was the peak allowable transmission amplitude level of an audio signal.

Y/C Recording   A method of recording in which the luminance information (Y) and the chrominance information (C) are recorded as separate tracks. They are combined at the output of the machine.

Index